This book should be returned to any branch of the
Lancashire County Library on or before the date shown

Lancashire County Library,
County Hall Complex,
1st floor Christ Church Precinct,
Preston, PR1 8XJ

www.lancashire.gov.uk/libraries

Lancashire
County
Council

LL1(A)

14 AMAZING PROJECTS YOU CAN MAKE TODAY!

Dr Alison Buxton
Director of STEAM Works

THIS IS A WELBECK CHILDREN'S BOOK

Published in 2019 by Welbeck Children's Bools, an imprint of the Welbeck Publishing Group, 20 Mortimer Street, London W1T 3JW

A catalogue record for this book is available from the British Library.

ISBN: 978 1 78312 523 4

Printed in Heshan, China

10 9 8 7 6 5 4 3 2 1

Writer: Dr Alison Buxton
Design Manager: Matt Drew
Design: Sam James and Andrew Thomas
Editorial Manager: Joff Brown
Production: Nicola Davey
Photographer: Simon Anning
Models: Evelyn Allan, Sharon Toren, Lona Cucos & Jenni Lazell

The publishers would like to thank the following sources for their kind permission to reproduce the pictures in this book.

Alamy: /Peter Atkinson: 84TL; /U.S. Department of Defense Archive: 105TL

Getty Images: /Thierry Falise/LightRocket: 36BR

Shutterstock: /Aaron Amat: 105BL; /AlexLMX: 36TR; /Andrey Eremin: 5TR, 10TL, 15BC; /Anteromite: 84BR; /Anton Starikov: 13R, 30L, 40C, 92R, 98C; /Dario Sabljak: 76TC; /Diego Cervo: 37TR; /Dmitri Ma: 61TR; /don padungvichean: 104B; /ESB Professional: 72TR; /except_else: 11T, 15BR; /Gruffi: 12-13BKG; /HQuality: 85L; /Ilona Belous: 73B; /IM_photo: 60TR; /indigolotos: 14BL; /invisible163: 14-15BKG; /Ioan Panaite: 10BL; /Jag_cz: 60B; /Jenson: 37BL; /Larina Marina: 85B; /Luba Shushpanova: 24L, 64C; /Mega Pixel: 4BR, 16TC, 17TR, 71BL, 71R; /mipan: 73TL; /Monkey Business Images: 104TC; /NDanko: 85R, 88TR; /Phonlamai Photo: 37BR; /photastic: 16R, 17TL, 20BC, 24C, 98C; /posteriori: 13TL, 61L, 72TL, 108TR; /prisma: 4BL, 5TL, 16TR, 16BR, 24TC, 68BR, 71BR, 106TR, 110; /Radmila: 14R; /Rawpixel.com: 85TR; /sathaporn: 2; /ScriptX: 14BR; /SeDmi: 13L; /sirastock: 10BR, 107TL, 107R; /Smile Fight: 61BR; /Tomislav Pinter: 12TR, 20TC, 30TC, 48R, 52R, 73TR, 98BC; /TSN52: 104TCR; /Triff: 104TR; /vchal: 104TL; /Vladimir Gjorgiev: 14L; /Wang An Qi: 72B; /Xinhua: 36BL; /Yellow Cat: 14BC; /Yurchanka Siarhei: 104TCL

Every effort has been made to acknowledge correctly and contact the source and/or copyright holder of each picture and Welbeck Publishing Group apologises for any unintentional errors or omissions that will be corrected in future editions of this book.

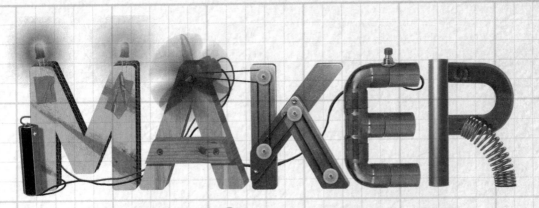

MAKER

WORKSHOP

14 AMAZING PROJECTS YOU CAN MAKE TODAY!

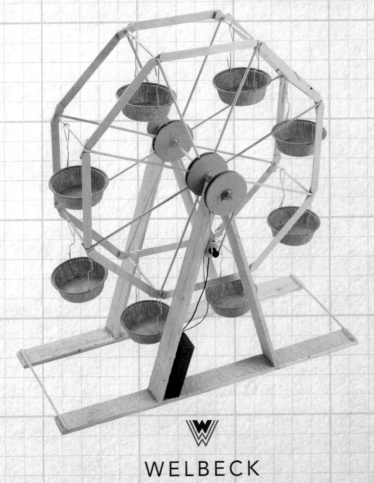

W

WELBECK

CONTENTS

Build!

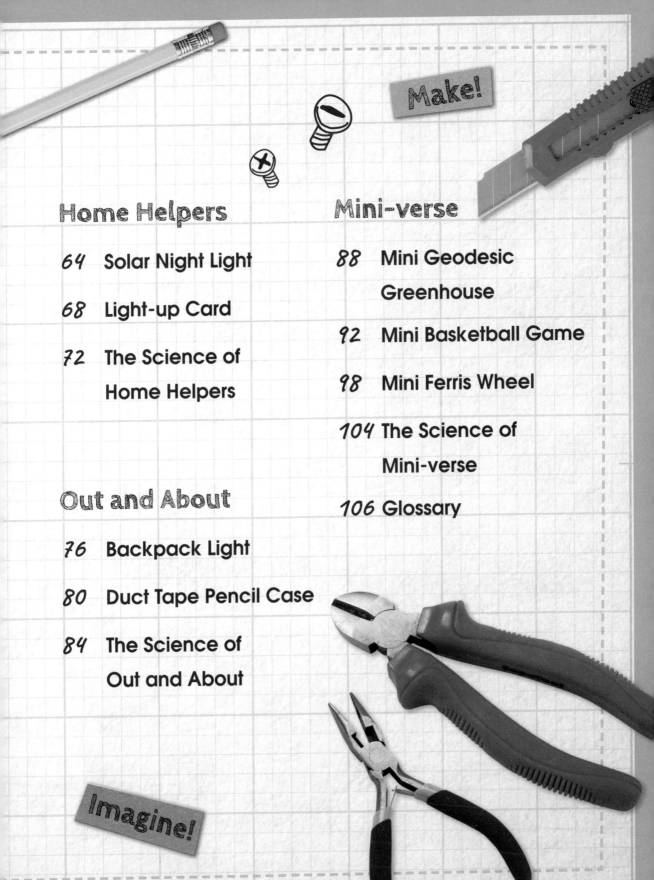

Make!

Home Helpers

Out and About

Mini-verse

Imagine!

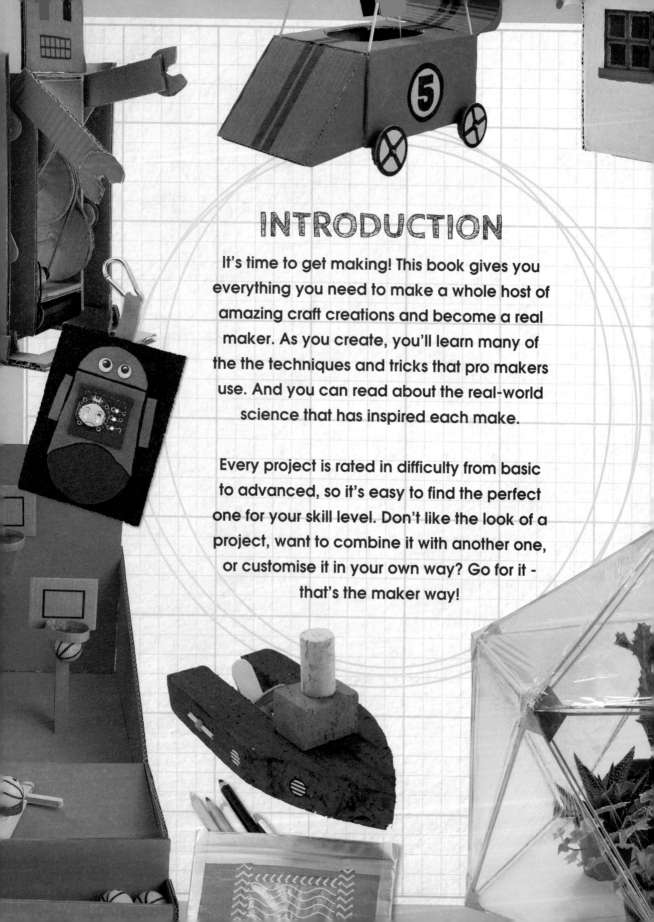

INTRODUCTION

It's time to get making! This book gives you everything you need to make a whole host of amazing craft creations and become a real maker. As you create, you'll learn many of the the techniques and tricks that pro makers use. And you can read about the real-world science that has inspired each make.

Every project is rated in difficulty from basic to advanced, so it's easy to find the perfect one for your skill level. Don't like the look of a project, want to combine it with another one, or customise it in your own way? Go for it - that's the maker way!

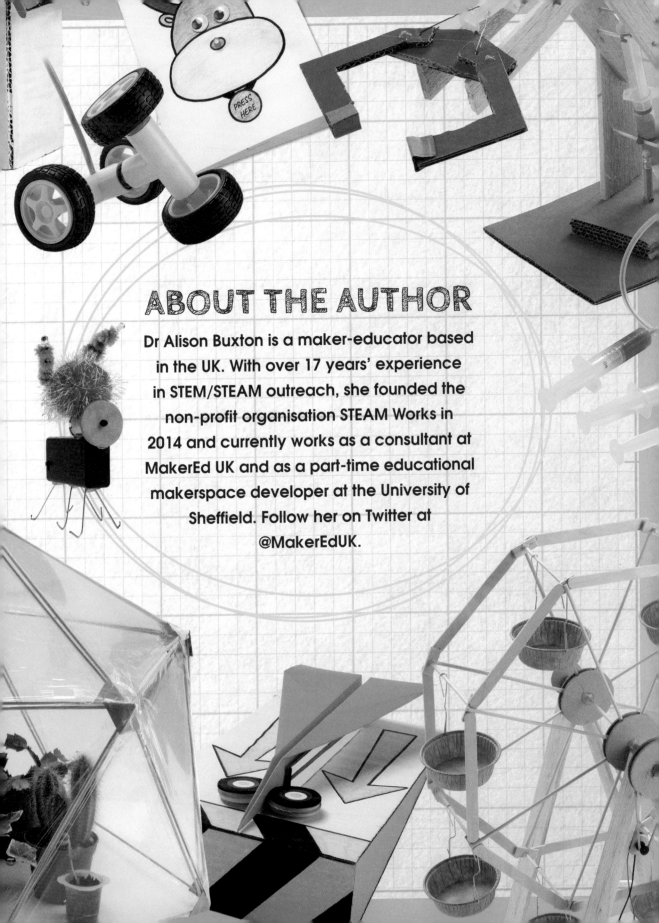

ABOUT THE AUTHOR

Dr Alison Buxton is a maker-educator based
in the UK. With over 17 years' experience
in STEM/STEAM outreach, she founded the
non-profit organisation STEAM Works in
2014 and currently works as a consultant at
MakerEd UK and as a part-time educational
makerspace developer at the University of
Sheffield. Follow her on Twitter at
@MakerEdUK.

TOOLS FOR THE JOB

THESE ARE THE MOST IMPORTANT TOOLS THAT ANY MAKER CAN USE. HOW MANY DO YOU HAVE?

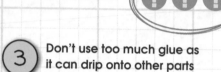

Hot glue gun

1 Let the gun heat up fully before you get gluing.

2 Glue guns sometimes drip when they are not being used, so use a mat or a stand to keep the drips off your worktop!

3 Don't use too much glue as it can drip onto other parts of your model.

4 Always have some spare glue sticks close at hand for when you run out.

5 Remember to switch off your glue gun when you have finished gluing.

⚠ THINK SAFE

The metal tip on a glue gun can get quite hot. Keep your fingers well away from the nozzle!

Pliers

1 Pliers are used for cutting, squishing and bending flexible but stiff materials, like metal and wire.

2 They can come in a variety of shapes to do different jobs, but the most useful for the makes in this book are needle-nose pliers and side cutters.

3 When cutting with pliers, get the flat side of the cutting edge up as close as possible to where you want to cut.

⚠ THINK SAFE

Cutting metal can leave sharp edges and metal splinters are harder to remove than wood ones! Always smooth down rough cut edges with sandpaper.

Bradawl

1 This hand tool is a bit like a screwdriver, but with a sharp point.

2 It is used for making pilot holes for screws, but also very useful for making holes in card and foam.

⚠ THINK SAFE

The sharp point is great for making holes, but keep your hands clear! Use a board or blob of putty behind your material to stop the bradawl scratching your worktop.

 ## Junior hacksaw

1 A junior hacksaw has a fine blade, making it ideal for cutting plastic or even very thin metal.

2 The blades can wear down quickly, but they're replaceable.

3 For extra stability, clamp the element you're cutting and use two hands on the saw - one on the handle and one on the top of the frame.

⚠ THINK SAFE

Be careful when replacing the blade on a junior hacksaw. The teeth should always be pointing away from the handle, and never force the blade into place.

4 When sawing, press down firmly and use small, pushing strokes.

Craft or precision knife

1 They are best used to cut really straight pieces of paper, card or duct tape.

2 These are knives with super sharp blades and great care needs to be taken with them.

⚠ THINK SAFE

Always use a cutting mat and raised steel ruler as a guide on a flat surface. Store your knife in a safe place. If the blade doesn't have a cover, you can use a cork or lump of modelling clay to cover the sharp bit.

Ask an adult to help!

Hand drills and bits

1 These have interchangeable ends of different sizes and for different materials called 'bits'.

2 Choose the size of the bit you need based on how big you want your hole.

3 Turn the handle clockwise to drill into wood, foam, plastic and metal.

⚠ THINK SAFE

Secure the item you are drilling in a vice to make sure it doesn't slip. Use a bradawl to make a pilot hole to help get you started.

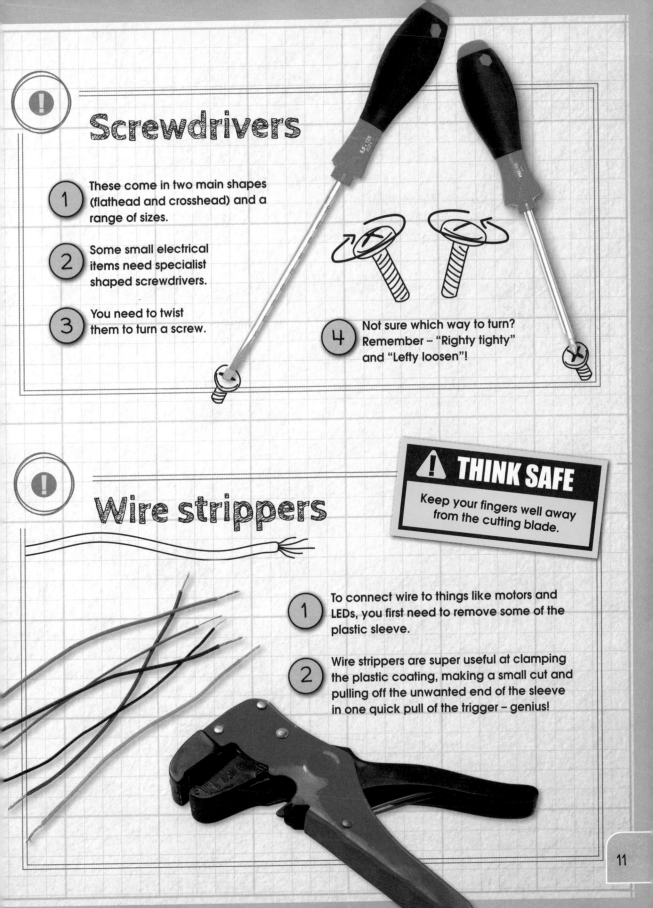

Screwdrivers

1 These come in two main shapes (flathead and crosshead) and a range of sizes.

2 Some small electrical items need specialist shaped screwdrivers.

3 You need to twist them to turn a screw.

4 Not sure which way to turn? Remember – "Righty tighty" and "Lefty loosen"!

Wire strippers

1 To connect wire to things like motors and LEDs, you first need to remove some of the plastic sleeve.

2 Wire strippers are super useful at clamping the plastic coating, making a small cut and pulling off the unwanted end of the sleeve in one quick pull of the trigger – genius!

YOUR MAKER KIT

MAKERS ARE ALWAYS COLLECTING USEFUL STUFF THEY CAN USE ON PROJECTS. HERE ARE SOME ESSENTIALS!

Batteries & holders

Batteries come in all sorts of shapes and sizes but can be tricky to use without a holder. 1.5v AA size and 3v coin cell batteries are really useful.

Wire

Multi-core wire is made up of lots of tiny strands of copper wire. Single core wire has just one thick piece. It's much easier to use single core wire for these projects.

Terminal blocks

Although a little bit bulky, these are a really helpful way to connect wires together.

Zip ties

These small plastic ties are a good way of connecting lengths of materials together.

LEDs

Light emitting diodes are a great way to brighten up your projects! Don't forget the long leg is positive and the short leg is negative.

Mini DC motor

Small electric motors run off two AA batteries, but if you want to go faster, try 4 AA batteries! Motors are measured in RPM – revs per minute. This is how many times the shaft spins all the way round in 1 minute. These motors have 12,000 RPM – that's a lot of spinning!

Tape

Electrical tape is perfect for binding wires – and adding colour to your makes.

Bamboo skewers, craft sticks & dowels

Don't have any wooden dowels? Bamboo sticks are a great alternative. They are pointed at one end so they can also be used to pierce holes on card and foam.

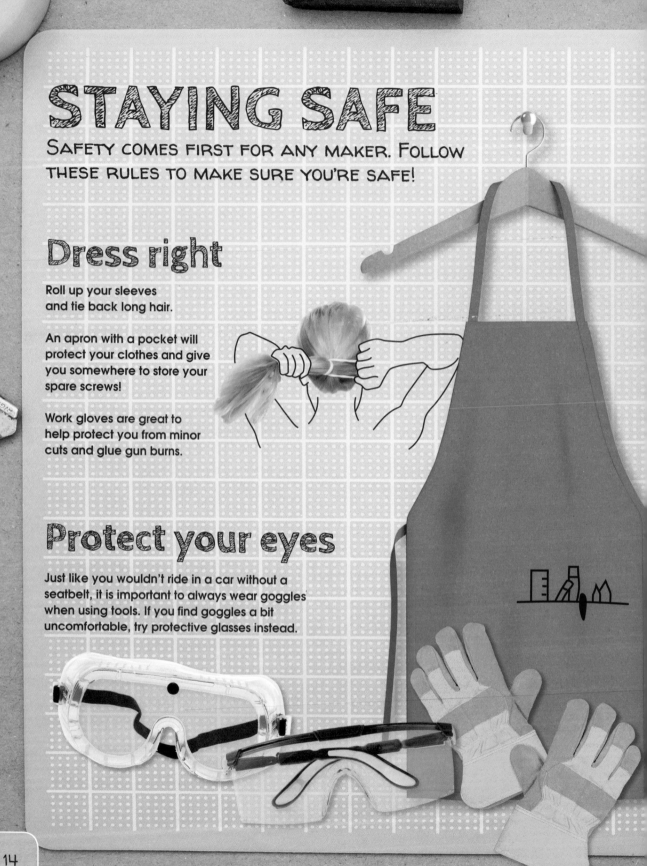

STAYING SAFE

SAFETY COMES FIRST FOR ANY MAKER. FOLLOW THESE RULES TO MAKE SURE YOU'RE SAFE!

Dress right

Roll up your sleeves and tie back long hair.

An apron with a pocket will protect your clothes and give you somewhere to store your spare screws!

Work gloves are great to help protect you from minor cuts and glue gun burns.

Protect your eyes

Just like you wouldn't ride in a car without a seatbelt, it is important to always wear goggles when using tools. If you find goggles a bit uncomfortable, try protective glasses instead.

Carry tools correctly

Be aware of who is around you and where you are taking your tools.

It is best to keep smaller tools such as screwdrivers and wires together in a small toolbox.

Point sharp bits down towards the floor.

Ask an adult to help!

Need adult supervision?

As you work through the projects, keep an eye out for this badge. Tools are safe if handled correctly, but it's always best to ask an adult to help out with tricky jobs.

Set up your workspace

Before you begin your project, check your working area is clear and set at a good working height with plenty of room for all of your supplies and tools.

Avoid ⚠ distractions

Try to find a quiet place to work so you can stay focused on the job at hand. A slip in focus might lead to a serious injury to you or someone else.

Right tool for the job

Always use the correct tool for the job you are trying to do.

It can be dangerous to try to use a tool for something it wasn't designed to do.

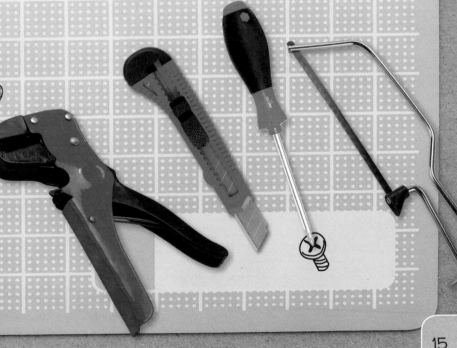

BECOMING A MAKER

MOST MAKERS AS WELL AS DESIGNERS, ENGINEERS AND OTHER CREATIVE FOLK FOLLOW A PROCESS LIKE THIS WHEN DOING ANY PROJECT.

Even when following instructions, things don't always go to plan.

As you progress, you might think of a way to improve a design or model.

The Maker Cycle gives you a framework to get you started, develop your ideas, make and test your design...

...and most importantly, see how you could improve it.

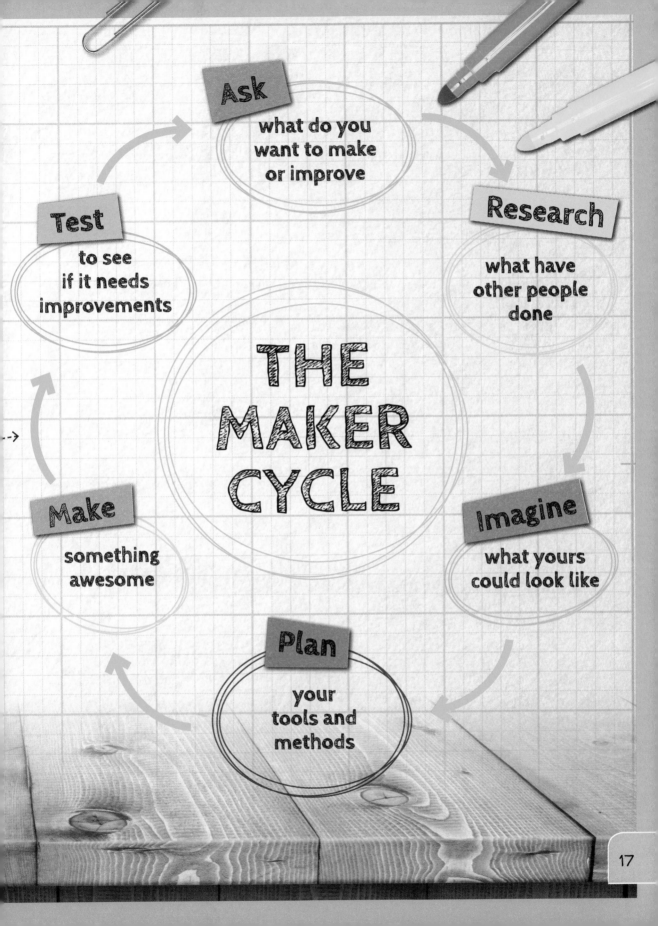

Ask
what do you want to make or improve

Research
what have other people done

Test
to see if it needs improvements

THE MAKER CYCLE

Imagine
what yours could look like

Make
something awesome

Plan
your tools and methods

BIONIC BOTS

Nothing's cooler than constructing your own working robot! Here are three amazing makes to inspire you.

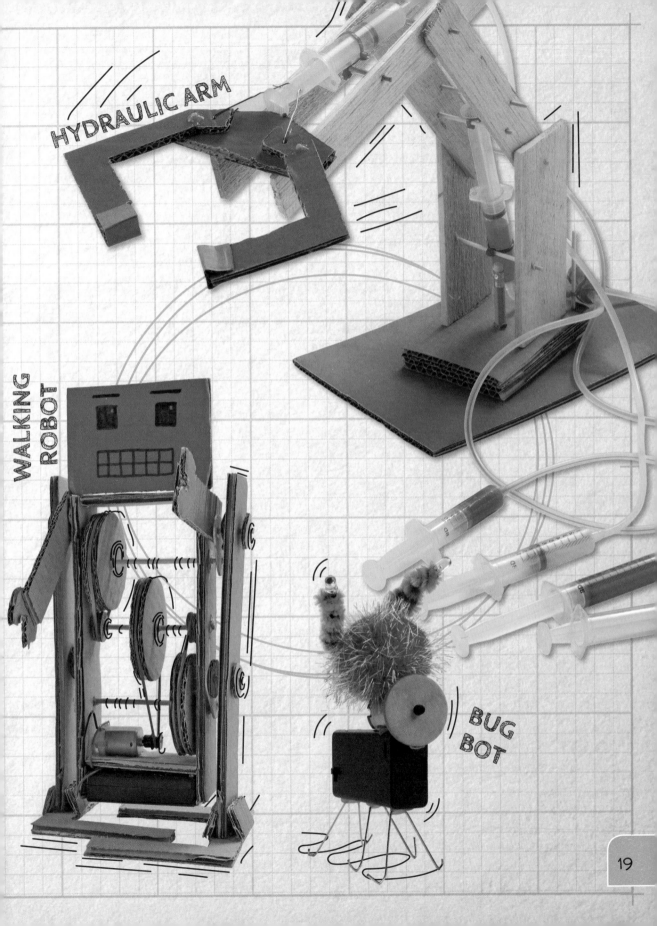

HYDRAULIC ARM

WALKING ROBOT

BUG BOT

19

BUG BOT

THIS LITTLE FELLA USES A WEIGHTED MOTOR TO JIG AND JITTER ACROSS A FLAT SURFACE. WHY NOT MAKE A WHOLE SWARM OF DIFFERENT ONES?

You will need:

Tools required:
- Hot glue gun
- Cutting mat
- Pliers
- Needle-nose pliers

2 x AA batteries

Motor

Shaft adaptor

AA Battery holder

Card disc

Cotton balls

Wired LEDs

Sticky putty

Pipe cleaners

Paper clips

Twist!

1

Make sure you have enough exposed wire at the end of the wired LEDs. Twist the two black LED wires together, then the two red wires.

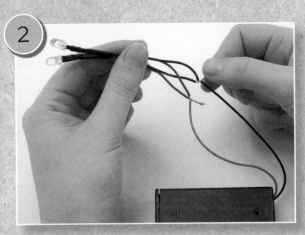

Connect the battery pack to the LEDs by twisting the black wire to the black LED wires, and the red wire to the red LED wires.

Connect!

Push the small plastic motor shaft adaptor onto the motor shaft.

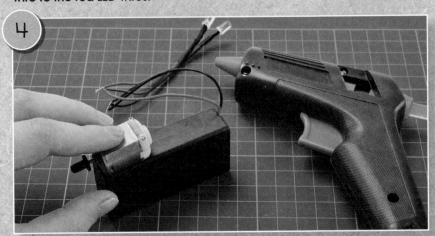

Glue the motor to the top of the AA battery pack. Make sure you only put the glue on the switch side, so you can still open the battery compartment!

Wrap!

Wrap pipe cleaners around the LED wires to create eyes on stalks. Choose whatever colour you like best to give your bug some character!

Connect the exposed wires to the motor. It doesn't matter which way round, because your bug will jitter whichever way the motor spins.

21

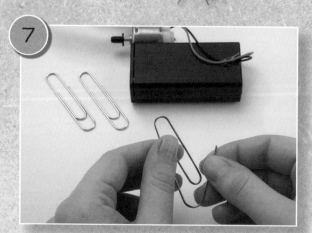

7 To make the legs, unbend three large paper clips.

8 Trim each paper clip with some side cutting pliers, at the points circled in the image.

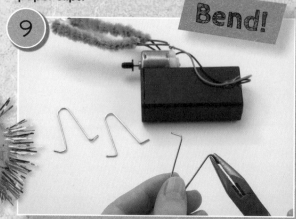

Bend!

9 Use a pair of needle-nose pliers to bend the cut ends into little feet.

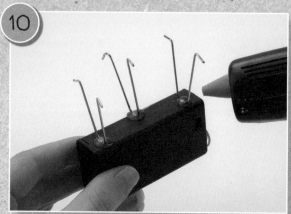

10 Turn the battery holder over and glue the legs in place on the underside. Glue two legs towards one side, and one leg towards the other side.

11 Add a small piece of sticky putty to the edge of the card disk. This will make the motor wobble.

Attach!

12 Push the disc onto the motor shaft. If it's not fitting tightly, secure it with a drop of glue.

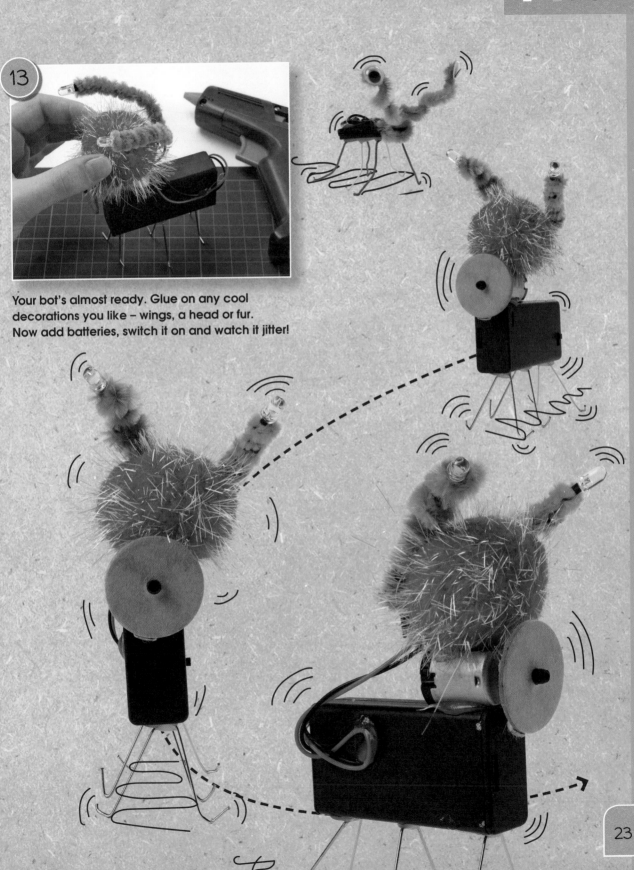

13

Your bot's almost ready. Glue on any cool decorations you like – wings, a head or fur. Now add batteries, switch it on and watch it jitter!

HYDRAULIC ARM

This robot arm doesn't use electricity — all its power comes from water pressure!

You will need:

Corrugated card

Pencil

Bamboo skewers

Paper clips

8 x 10ml syringes

Poster paint

14 x small zip ties

2m of clear flexible tubing that fits the syringes

Balsa wood

Tools required:

- Bradawl
- Side cutting pliers
- Pencil
- Hot glue gun
- Hand drill

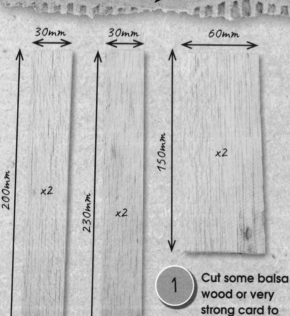

30mm 30mm 60mm

200mm x2

230mm x2

150mm x2

1 Cut some balsa wood or very strong card to the sizes shown here.

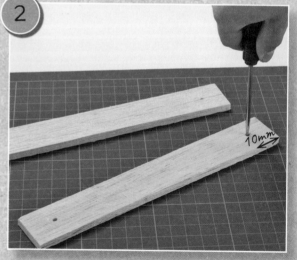

10mm

Take the 200mm long pieces, and use a bradawl to pierce a central hole approximately 10mm from each end on both pieces.

2

Pinch!

3

6cm

Now take the two 230mm arm pieces, and pierce holes 10mm in from each end and another hole 60mm in from the end.

4

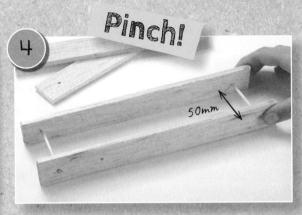

50mm

Cut a 50mm piece of skewer using your pliers, and insert it through the two end holes.

5

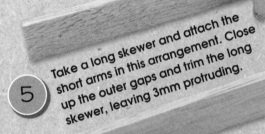

Take a long skewer and attach the short arms in this arrangement. Close up the outer gaps and trim the long skewer, leaving 3mm protruding.

Snip!

7

6

Take the two remaining pieces of balsa and use the bradawl to make a central hole in the top of both pieces, about 15mm down. These will be your support walls.

Insert a skewer through the first support wall, then through the holes in the two shorter arm pieces followed by the second support wall. Trim off the excess, leaving 3mm. Glue each joint in place.

8

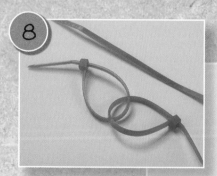

Pull!

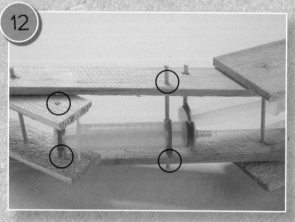

To make the fixings for the hydraulics, link together two zip ties into a figure of eight.

Slip one of the loops onto the top of the syringe and tighten.

Insert a short length of skewer, approximately 60mm, through the remaining loop and tighten.

9

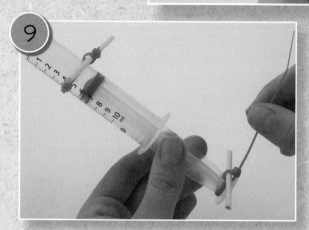

Repeat the process to attach a second skewer to the base of the syringe.

10

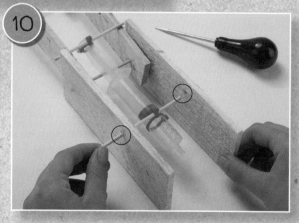

Position the top of the first syringe about halfway down the support wall, by making a hole for the skewer through both walls.

11

Pull the syringe nearly all the way out, to see where on the short arm it reaches. Mark the point and make the holes for the skewer, then slide the skewer in as shown.

12

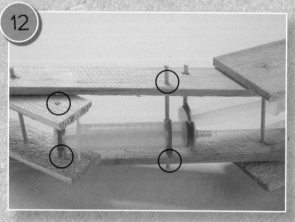

Make up another identical syringe, and connect the base of the plunger to the upper holes in the arm as shown. Form new holes towards the bottom of the forearm for the top of the syringe.

13

To make the platform for your arm, cut out two pieces of cardboard 120mm by 90mm and glue them together to make a thick rectangle.

14

Use a pencil to pierce a hole through the middle of the platform.

15

Snip!

Cut the blunt end of the pencil to 50mm length, as shown.

16

Cut a 250mm by 150mm sheet of card, and hot glue the pencil in the middle. Slide the platform onto the pencil - but only when the glue has set!

17

Glue!

Use the hot glue gun to secure the two support walls onto the platform. The whole platform should be able to rotate freely on the base plate.

18

Make up another syringe, and make a small hole in the right corner of the back of the platform. Insert and glue the skewer at the base of the syringe. Turn the platform left, and place the top of the syringe to the back left corner of the base. Secure the skewer pin with a spot of glue.

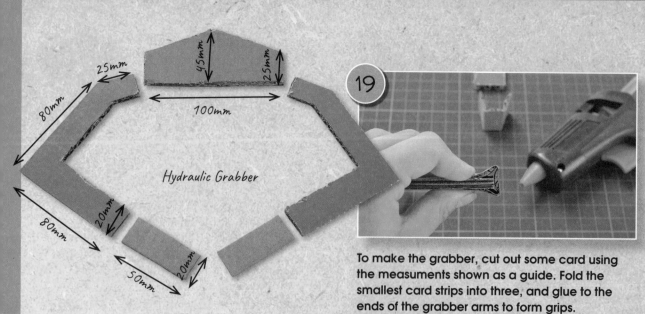

25mm

80mm

45mm

25mm

100mm

20mm

80mm

Hydraulic Grabber

20mm

50mm

20mm

19

To make the grabber, cut out some card using the measuments shown as a guide. Fold the smallest card strips into three, and glue to the ends of the grabber arms to form grips.

19

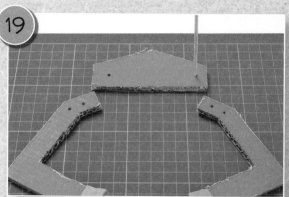

Make small holes in the positions shown above, and insert a skewer in the two holes on the topmost section.

21

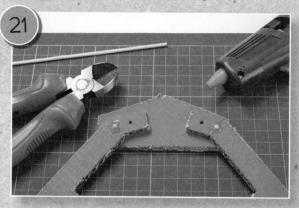

Thread the arms onto the skewers as shown. Trim and glue the exposed skewer ends on one side only, so the arms can rotate freely.

22

Bend!

Take two large paperclips and straighten out the large loop so they still have the smaller loops to act as hooks. Keep them to hand, you will need them in a bit...

23

Drill!

Ask an adult to help!

Prepare the last syringe by adding one zip tie and skewer fixing to the top end, and attach this half way up the tube. Drill two small holes in the end of the plunger as shown.

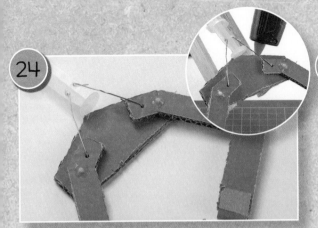

24 Thread the paperclip hooks through the ends of the grabber arms. Now hot glue the grabber to the end of the arm.

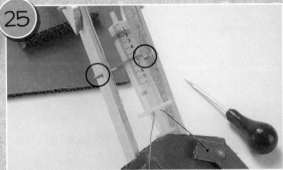

25 Use a bradawl to make holes where the skewer lines up on the arm, and fix in place.

26 Cut the plastic tubing into four equal lengths ,and attach to the syringes on your model. Make sure all the syringes on your robotic arm are pushed into their closed positions.

27 Mix poster paint or food colouring with water to make four different coloured waters. Fill the four syringes each with a different coloured water and attach them to the other end of the tubing.

Play!

28 To operate your hydraulic arm, push and pull on the control syringes and watch it come alive!

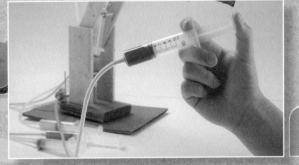

WALKING ROBOT

WITH THE HELP OF SOME CLEVER GEARS, THIS CARDBOARD ROBOT USES A SINGLE MOTOR TO WALK BY ITSELF!

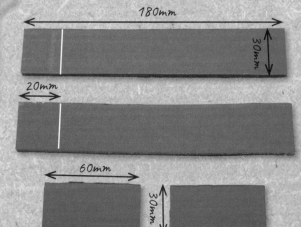

You will need:

2 x AA batteries

Corrugated cardboard

Pulley

Electric motor

Straws

Elastic bands

Craft Sticks

AA battery pack with switch

Bamboo skewers

Tools required:
- Hot glue gun
- Cutting mat
- Scissors
- Pencil
- Pliers
- Bradawl or hand drill

1 Make the sides of your robot by cutting out two pieces of corrugated cardboard 180mm by 30mm, and mark a vertical line 20mm in from one end. Then cut out two smaller pieces, as shown below.

180mm

30mm

20mm

60mm

30mm

2

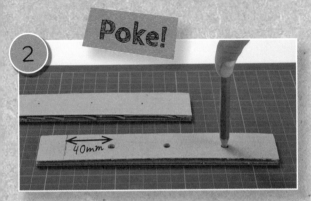

Poke!

Use a pencil to mark three small holes at 40mm intervals between the vertical line and the other end of the strip. Use the pencil to make each of the holes just wide enough to fit a plastic straw.

3

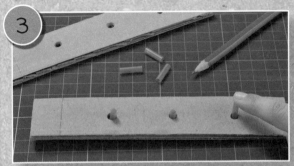

Cut the straw into six 10mm lengths, and push one through each of the holes.

4

Glue!

Turn the card over and use a glue gun to secure each piece in place. Be careful not to block the straws with glue!

5

Take your small card rectangles and glue the top and bottom pieces to the side pieces to form your robot's body. Make sure the bottom piece is placed on the line 20mm from the end.

6

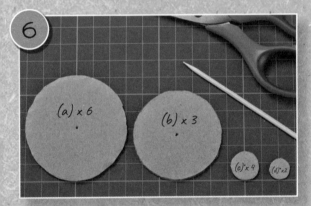

Cut six cardboard 60mm diameter circles (a), three cardboard 55mm diameter circles (b), four 10mm diameter circles (c) and two 5mm diameter circles (d). Mark the centre point of each circle and pierce with a bamboo skewer.

7

Skewer!

To create your first pulley, cut a skewer 65mm long and thread the circles on in this order: c, d, c, a, b, a, c, d, c. It should look like the image above.

Now cut two pieces of bamboo skewer 80mm long and create two more pulleys using this configuration: a, b, a. Hot glue all the pulleys together to look like the above picture.

10 Carefully line up the top and bottom large pulleys with the small pulleys in the middle by sliding them along the skewers. Stretch the elastic bands from the top and bottom pulleys around the small ones.

Place an elastic band around the centre of the three large pulleys before inserting the skewers into your robot's body.

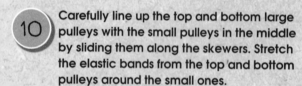

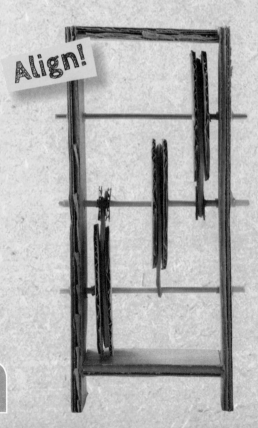

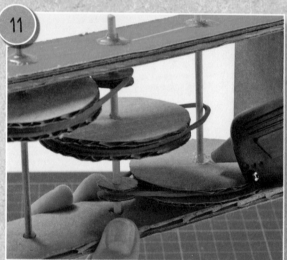

Once they are lined up, glue each pulley to the skewer.

12

Connect a small plastic pulley to the shaft of the motor.

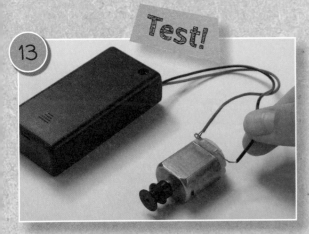

13

Test!

Connect the battery pack to the motor by twisting each wire from the battery pack round a terminal at the base of the motor. Insert the batteries to test the motor.

14

Hook the elastic band from the central pulley around the motor's pulley. Glue the motor into place at the base of your robot's body. Now glue the battery pack under the base of your robot, making sure you don't block the switch or the lid.

15

Snip!

To make the mechanism for the legs, cut craft sticks into four 30mm pieces, and carefully round the ends of each one. Use a bradawl or drill to make a small hole at each end of the sticks.

16

Cut a skewer into four 20mm lengths and insert each piece about 1mm through a hole in each of the craft sticks. Glue these into place.

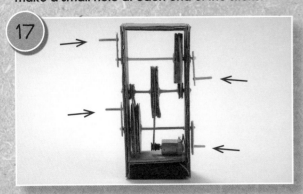

17

Thread the pieces onto the top and bottom skewers outside the body. Make sure the pieces on the right side are turned upwards, and the pieces on the left are turned down.

18

Use a small amount of glue to secure these to the skewers, and trim off any excess skewer.

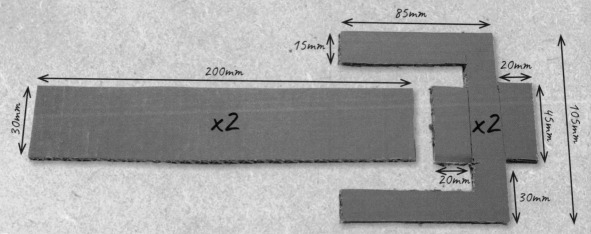

85mm

15mm

200mm

20mm

30mm

x2

105mm

45mm

x2

20mm

20mm

30mm

19 To make the legs of your robot, cut out two 200mm x 30mm strips of cardboard.

20 To make the feet, form two shapes like a large letter E out of cardboard, as shown.

21

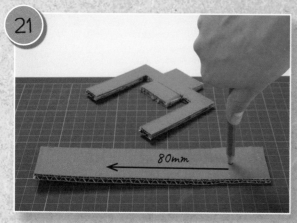

80mm

Use a pencil to make a central hole near the top of each leg. Make a second hole 80mm below it.

22

Attach the legs to the feet by bending up the central flaps and gluing them to the legs.

23

Cut out eight small cardboard discs about 10mm wide, and pierce a small hole in each one. Place these onto the mechanism skewers.

24

Place the legs onto your robot body.

Slide the remaining cardboard discs onto the exposed skewers and secure with hot glue, making sure the skewers can still rotate.

 Now decorate your robot however you like. Add a head and arms with a cool robotic feel.

 Hit the switch and watch your robot walk! You may need to reposition the legs if they unbalance the robot.

THE SCIENCE OF BIONIC BOTS

Robot heroes

Some of the most useful robots are developed to do the jobs that might be too dangerous for humans. Explosive ordnance disposal (EOD) or bomb-disposal robots are used to disarm improvised explosive devices (IEDs). They are fitted with sensors, cameras and an arm-like manipulator, and are controlled by a human operative working at a safe distance.

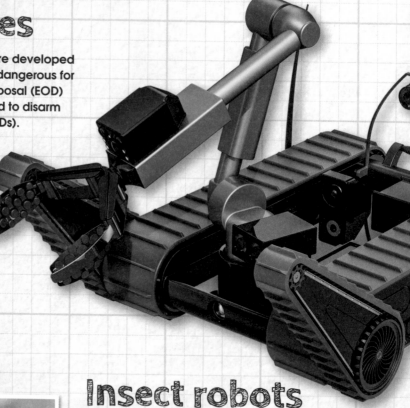

Insect robots

With bee populations in decline, robots are being developed that mimic the role of insects! RoboBees, developed by Harvard University, are about the size of regular bees and use tiny wings to fly. The aim is to develop a fully autonomous swarm of robots capable of artificial pollination as well as spying and even search and rescue capabilities!

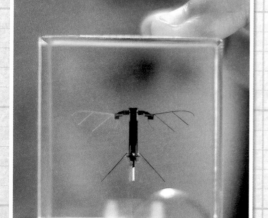

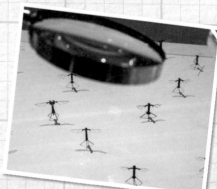

Home help robots

Think a robot to help with your household chores would be nice? Well, they do exist! Vacuum robots first came onto the consumer market in 1996, but the first Robotic Vacuum Cleaner struggled to navigate around objects and get into hard to reach places. In 2002, a superior floor-cleaning robot was launched that had sensors allowing it to change direction if it encountered an object and detect dirty patches. Time to put your feet up!

Robotic arms

Robotic arms are used widely across the world... and even in space. They have made many types of manufacturing much easier and quicker. Some robotic arms use hydraulics (like the water-powered arm on page 24), and others use motors to move. They are good at placing and rotating heavy parts such as cars, or small precision movements such as tightening screws.

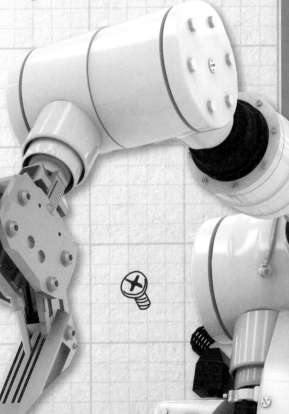

MEGA MOVERS

THESE SUPER-SPEEDY
INVENTIONS CAN TRAVEL OVER
LAND, AIR OR WATER!

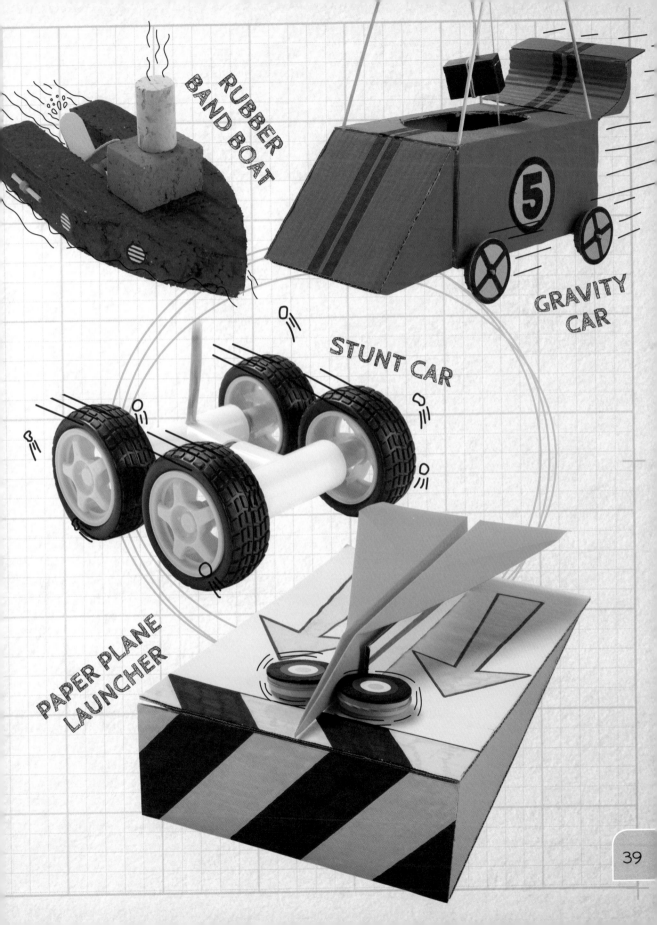

RUBBER
BAND BOAT

GRAVITY
CAR

⑤

STUNT CAR

PAPER PLANE
LAUNCHER

39

RUBBER BAND BOAT

THIS SIMPLE BOAT USES THE STORED POWER OF A WOUND-UP ELASTIC BAND TO WHIZZ ACROSS WATER.

You will need:

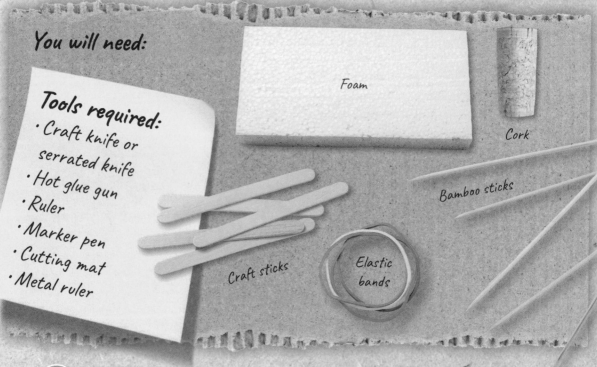

Tools required:
- Craft knife or serrated knife
- Hot glue gun
- Ruler
- Marker pen
- Cutting mat
- Metal ruler

Foam

Cork

Bamboo sticks

Craft sticks

Elastic bands

1

Take a piece of foam approximately 100 x 180mm. Shape the front of the boat by drawing an arc from the centre point at one end to approximately half way along the long edge, as shown.

2

Ask an adult to help!

Use a serrated knife or craft knife to carefully cut along the curve.

3

Turn the off-cut over and use it draw a mirror image of the first line. Cut out the second arc too.

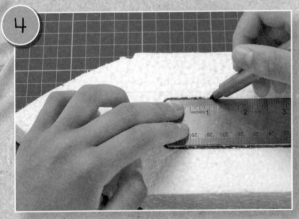

4

Centre a ruler about 70mm in at the back of the boat. Draw around it to form a long rectangle.

5

Cut out the rectangle and then chop about 1/3 off the end.

6

Take the larger piece and glue it to the top of the boat near the front to form a cabin. Then glue a cork on top to make the funnel.

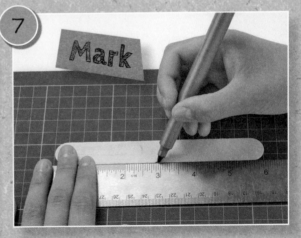

7

Mark

Take a thick craft stick and mark the centre.

8

Use a large pair of scissors to cut the craft stick in half and round off the ends.

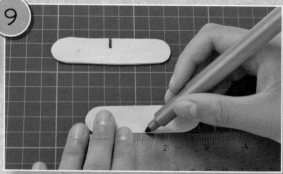

9

Use a ruler to mark the halfway point. Draw a line halfway across each of the short sticks.

10

Use scissors to carefully cut out a slit on both sticks.

11

Connect!

Slot the two short sticks together to form an X and secure with a small amount of hot glue. This is the paddle that will help drive the boat.

12

Put the paddle in the cut-out, making sure it's not touching the boat at the front. Insert a skewer through the boat's side, in line with the paddle's centre.

Remove the paddle and push the skewer though the far side of the boat. Give the skewer a wiggle to enlarge the hole.

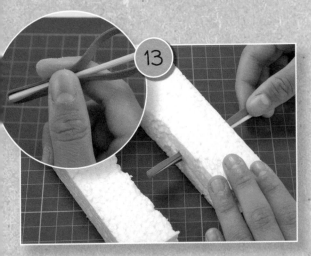

Remove the skewer and place an elastic band over the blunt end. Use the end of the skewer to thread the band through the holes.

Once the band is all the way through, remove the skewer and cut off two short lengths. Thread them through the end loops of the band on either side of the boat to hold it in place, as shown.

Thread the paddle through the elastic band.

 Paint your boat brightly, then wind up the paddle tightly. Place your boat in water before releasing the paddle, and watch it go!

GRAVITY POWERED CAR

NO MOTORS, WIRES OR BATTERIES NEEDED HERE — THIS CAR RUNS ON THE POWER OF A FALLING WEIGHT!

You will need:

4 x milk bottle tops

Cardboard discs

Heavy weight

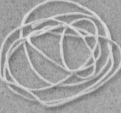

Bamboo skewers

String

3 x straws

Tools required:
- Knife
- Cutting Mat
- Hot glue gun
- Pliers
- Scissors

---

1 Take a small cardboard box and open it out so it is flat.

Small cardboard box

2

Glue!

Turn the box inside out and secure back together with hot glue.

Draw a small rectangle about 10mm from one end on the base of the box. Cut this out with a knife or scissors.

Ask an adult to help!

Turn the box over and draw a large oval on the top of the box and cut it out. This is the top of your gravity powered car.

Pierce each corner with a skewer.
Push each skewer about 20mm into the box.

Bend!

Take a straw and cut it into two 50mm lengths and bend a piece of straw in half.

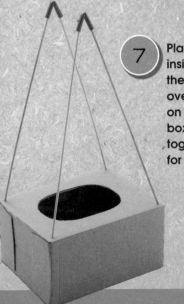

Place a little hot glue inside each end. Slide the ends of the straw over the two skewers on one side of the box to join them together. Repeat this for the other side.

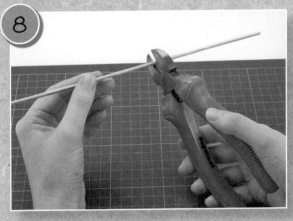

Cut a piece of skewer slightly shorter than the width of the box.

Glue the skewer securely on top of the straws.

Glue a straw over the rectangle opening on the base and another at the bottom. Make sure the straws are parallel or your wheels won't work!

Use scissors to snip away the area of straw that lies over the small rectangular hole and trim the ends of the straws, with an overhang of 3mm.

Take four plastic milk bottle tops and use a skewer to pierce a hole in the centre of each wheel. Then glue the card disc on the bottle tops.

Thread a wheel onto a skewer and then push the skewer through one of the straw axle holders, before adding a second wheel.

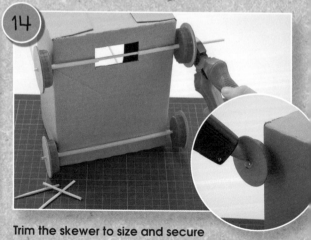

Trim the skewer to size and secure the wheels to the skewer with hot glue.

15

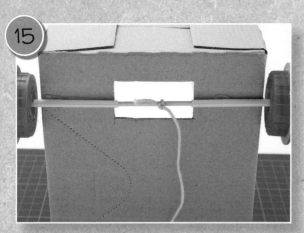

Take a long piece of string and tie it to the axle below the hole in the base. Feed the rest of the string through the hole.

16

Loop the string over the rail at the top of the model and attach your heavy weight to the end of the string.

17

Wind!

Paint your vehicle in racing colours. When it's dry, wind the axel until all of the slack is taken up in the string and the weight is at the top rail. Release the weight and watch your car accelerate with the power of gravity!

Race!

47

PAPER PLANE LAUNCHER

USE TWO ELECTRIC MOTORS TO CREATE THE
ULTIMATE PAPER PLANE LAUNCHER — YOU
WON'T BELIEVE HOW FAST THEY'LL GO!

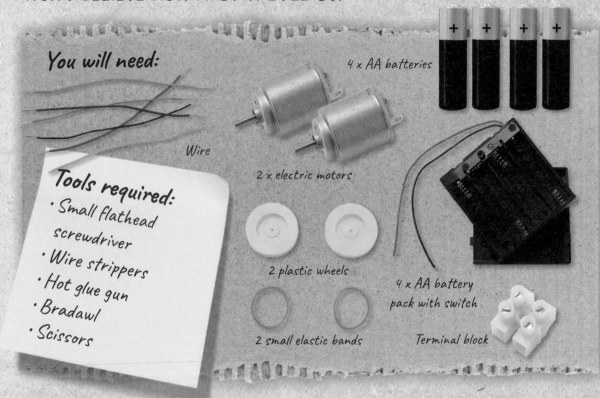

You will need:

4 x AA batteries

Wire

2 x electric motors

2 plastic wheels

4 x AA battery
pack with switch

2 small elastic bands

Terminal block

Tools required:
- Small flathead screwdriver
- Wire strippers
- Hot glue gun
- Bradawl
- Scissors

1   Cut out some corrugated card
    to the measurements shown below.

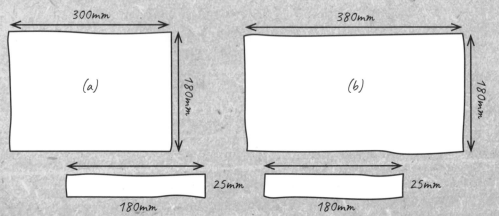

300mm

180mm

(a)

380mm

180mm

(b)

180mm · 25mm

180mm · 25mm

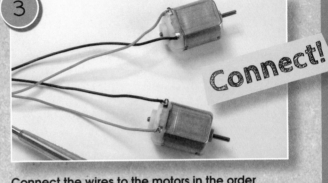

Connect!

Cut two pieces of red wire 120mm long and use wire strippers to remove 5mm of plastic from each end. Repeat this with the black wire so you have two pieces of each.

Connect the wires to the motors in the order shown by threading the exposed wire ends through the points on the back of the motor and twist the wire back on itself to secure.

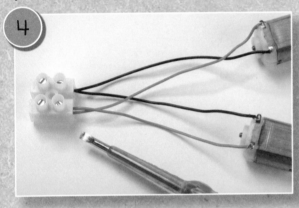

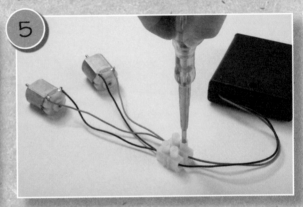

Insert the two red wires into one point in the terminal block and the two black wires into the second point. Screw the connections tight.

Insert the red wire from the battery box into the terminal behind the red motor wires and the black wire into the other terminal and tighten.

Mark!

Take the thin piece of corrugated card (a) and position the two wheels about 50mm from the top with a gap of 3mm between them.

Remove the wheels and use a bradawl to make the holes bigger.

8

Push the shaft of each motor through the holes and use a hot glue gun to secure each motor into place.

Glue!

9

Take two plastic wheels and carefully wrap an elastic band around each one. This helps to provide more friction.

10

Push the wheels on to the motor shafts.

Bend!

11 To make the base of the frame, take a piece of card (b) and use a sharp edge to score and fold the card 80mm from the end.

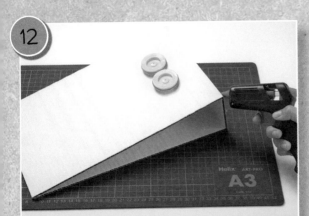

12 Glue the launcher onto the folded card so it is angled upwards.

13 Glue the two strips of card onto the launcher about 5mm apart and just below the wheels. Now decorate the launcher however you like.

14 Switch the motors on and launch a paper plane down the groove... WHOOSH!

51

STUNT CAR

Can you really make your own remote-controlled stunt car? Follow these instructions and you can!

You will need:

Tools required:
- Hand drill
- Hot glue gun
- Wire strippers
- Junior hacksaw
- Bradawl
- Scissors

3 x motors

Cork

4 x AA batteries

Electrical tape

2 switches

9 metres of wire

Terminal block

4 x RC car wheels

6 colours of wire

Straw

Corrugated Cardboard

2 x plastic tee joints

4 AA battery holder

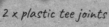

1

Drill!

Ask an adult to help!

Take a plastic tee joint and use a hand drill to carefully make a hole wide enough for the straw in the centre of one side.

2

Cut 6 pieces of wire 100mm long and strip about 5mm of insulation off each end. If you don't have 6 different coloured wires, number each wire 1-6 top and bottom with a piece of masking tape.

Car wiring diagram

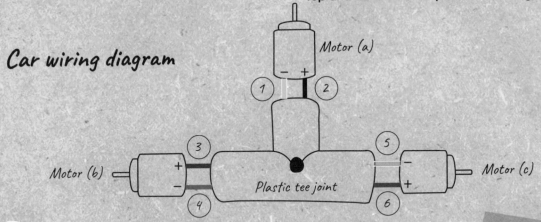

Motor (a)

− +

1   2

Motor (b)

+   −

3

4

Plastic tee joint

5

−   +

6

Motor (c)

3

Plan!

Secure two wires to each motor by threading the end of one wire through the positive terminal hole and the second through the negative terminal hole on the bottom of the motor. Hook and twist the wire back on itself to secure. Use the diagram above to help you.

Motor (a)

Motor (c)

Motor (b)

53

4

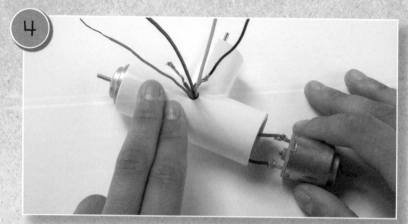

Place motor (a) in the top of the tee joint and thread the wires through the hole in the centre. Repeat this for motors (b) and (c) and place them in the remaining holes in the tee joint. The motors need to be a really tight fit, so you might need to use tape, cardboard strips or glue to pack out motors so they are really secure and don't twist or move about in the holes.

5

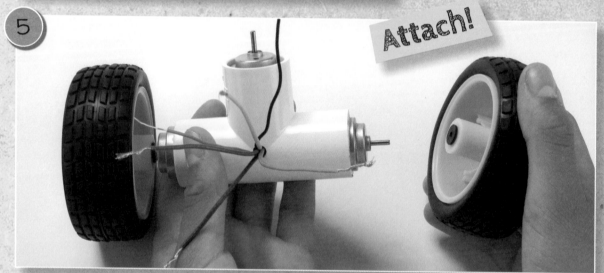

Attach!

Fit a pair of wheels to motors (b) & (c) to form the rear of the car.

6 Refer back to your wiring diagram and connect the positive (+) wire (3) from motor (b) to the negative (-) wire (5) of motor (c) by twisting the ends of the wire together. Cover the connection with some electrical tape. Repeat this process with the negative wire (4) on motor (b) and the positive wire (6) on motor (c).

Twist!

Saw!

7

Ask an adult to help!

Carefully cut a cork into three equal pieces using a small hacksaw.

8

Carefully drill a hole as wide as a straw down the centre of two of the corks.

9

Take the second tee joint and thread a straw through one cork piece, then slide the straw through the opposing openings. Slide the second piece of cork on the end of the straw.

10 Glue the corks in place using a hot glue gun and trim off any excess straw.

55

Snip!

10

Slide a wooden skewer through the straw-lined holes and trim it down so only 8mm of skewer is sticking out each side. Push a wheel onto each axle and glue in place. This is the front of the car.

11

Make a hole with a bradawl very slightly smaller than the motor shaft through the centre of the last piece of cork.

12

Push the motor shaft into this hole – this should be a very tight fit. If it is not super tight, add a bit of glue.

13

Bring the both sides of the car together and secure with glue.

Nice!

Now on to the control unit...

Connect!

Cut a shape out of cardboard to use as the base of your controller. It needs to be big enough to mount the battery pack and wiring on the back.

Fix the two switches 20-30mm in from each side of your controller, so you can easily reach them with your thumbs.

Fix the red wire and black wire into the terminal block.

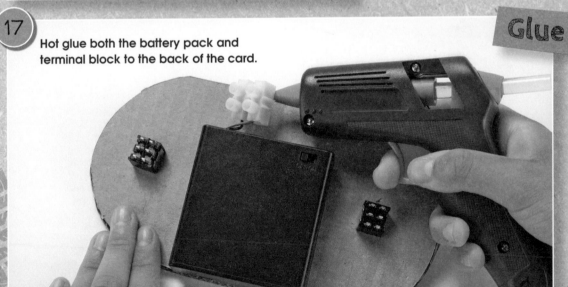

Hot glue both the battery pack and terminal block to the back of the card.

Glue

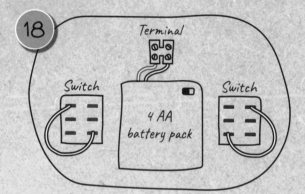

Loop a small length of wire in the left switch box from top left to bottom right. On the right switch box, loop wire from top right to bottom left.

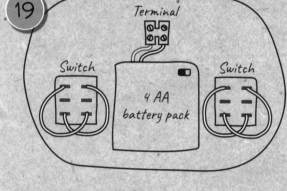

Now repeat, with the wires running from top right to bottom left on the left switch, and top left to bottom right on the right switch.

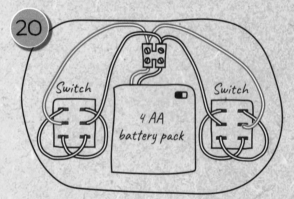

Secure two red and two black wires to the terminal, then attach them to the centre slots of the switches as shown.

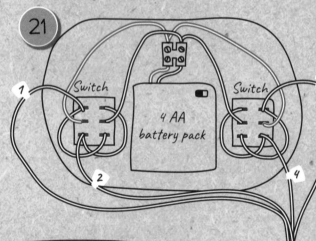

Thread all of the long wires through a straw before connecting them to the motor wires as shown.

Connect the wires by twisting them together and secure the joints. Use the above diagram to help you.

Twist!

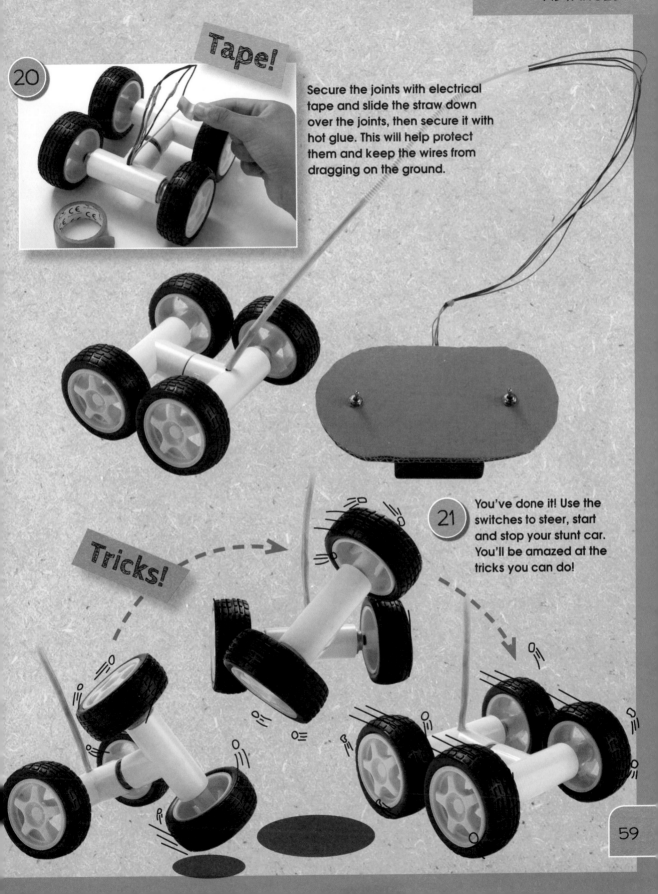

Tape!

20

Secure the joints with electrical tape and slide the straw down over the joints, then secure it with hot glue. This will help protect them and keep the wires from dragging on the ground.

21 You've done it! Use the switches to steer, start and stop your stunt car. You'll be amazed at the tricks you can do!

Tricks!

THE SCIENCE OF MEGA MOVERS

How planes fly

Ever wondered how something as heavy as a jumbo jet can actually fly? Planes don't have to have an engine to fly, but they do need to be travelling at speed.

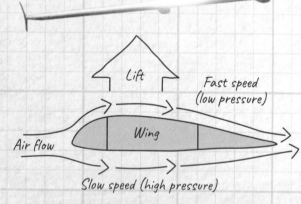

Lift

Fast speed (low pressure)

Air flow

Wing

Slow speed (high pressure)

The secret to flight is in the shape of the wings. Once a plane is travelling fast enough, the air hits the wings and changes its direction and pressure, causing lift. Once the lift becomes greater than the weight of the plane, it takes off!

How a remote control works

Early remote controls were wired like the one on your stunt car, but how do modern remote controls work without wires? The remote control sends out pulses of infrared light from an LED that represent specific binary codes for functions such as on/off or volume up/down. The light is invisible to us, but the object receiving the code, such as your TV, can see it.

Electric motors

Your gravity-powered car isn't the only vehicle that doesn't need petrol. More and more cars are using electric motors as a greener, more efficient power source than fossil fuels. An electric engine takes power from a large rechargeable battery which powers a series of electric motors to drive the wheels and things like the power steering and lights.

HOME HELPERS

THESE COOL INVENTIONS ARE
PERFECT FOR MAKING AT HOME
OR USING AS GIFTS!

SOLAR
NIGHT LIGHT

PRESS
HERE

LIGHT-UP
GREETINGS CARD

63

SOLAR NIGHT LIGHT

RE-USE AN OLD GARDEN SOLAR LIGHT TO MAKE A NIGHT LIGHT HOUSE THAT ONLY TURNS ON WHEN IT GETS DARK.

You will need:

Solar garden light with switch

Tools required:
- Hot glue gun
- Cutting mat
- Craft knife
- Metal ruler
- Marker pen

A selection of paints

Corrugated card

120mm 70mm 120mm 70mm

120mm

1 Draw a series of four adjoining rectangles onto card.

Plan!

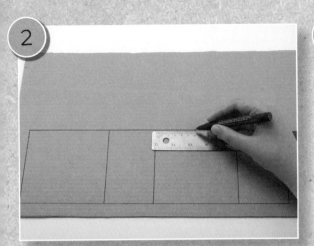

2

Mark the middle point along the top of the two larger squares.

3

Measure!

Measure 100mm above the square to give you the tip of the roof point.

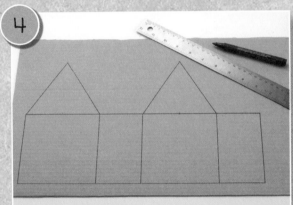

4

Connect the corner of each large square to the roof tip point to form two triangles.

5

Ask an adult to help!

Cut!

Using a craft knife or card cutter, carefully cut around the outer shape.

6

Score!

Score lightly along the vertical lines, being careful not to cut all the way through.

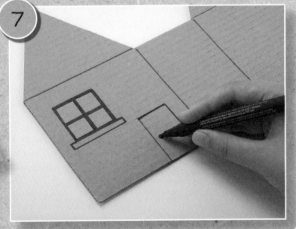

7

Add a door and window to the first square. This will be the front of the house.

65

Ask an adult to help!

Cut the window and then the door so it can be opened. This will allow your light to shine out.

Take a solar garden light and remove the top containing the solar cell, LED and switch.

10

Draw around the top of the light on the second large square panel.

11

Ask an adult to help!

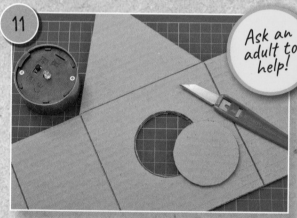

Cut out to form a hole. Be careful not to cut your hole too big!

12

Push!

Push the light through the hole, so the solar cell is facing outwards.

13

Bend the house template along the scored lines and use a hot glue gun to connect the two outer edges to form a 3D house.

Ask an adult to help!

14

Cut out a piece of cardboard to 80x300mm.
Score and fold down the middle to form a roof.

15

Use hot glue to attach the roof to the house.

16 Paint your house in whatever
colours you like. Place your solar
night light on a sunny window sill
during the day and it will emit light
after dark. Don't forget to turn the
switch on!

HOW IT WORKS

The solar cell collects
energy from the sun and
charges through the day.
A light sensor keeps the
light turned off while it is
daylight and turns the light
on only when it is dark.

LIGHT-UP GREETINGS CARD

THIS FUN, FUNKY CARD WILL REALLY LIGHT UP A FRIEND OR FAMILY MEMBER'S DAY. WE'VE MADE A FESTIVE CARD, BUT YOU COULD MAKE A BIRTHDAY CARD TOO!

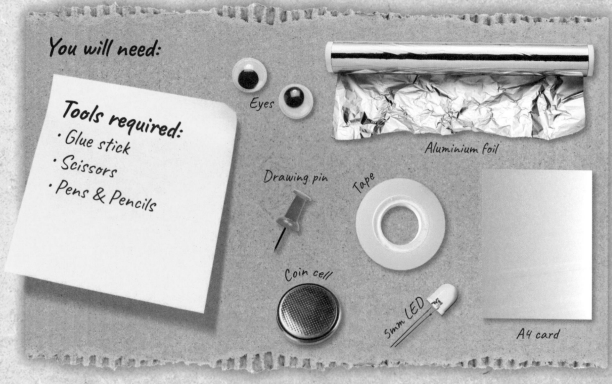

You will need:

Tools required:
- Glue stick
- Scissors
- Pens & Pencils

Eyes

Aluminium foil

Drawing pin

Tape

Coin cell

5mm LED

A4 card

1

Design!

Fold the piece of card down the middle and draw a design on the front. In your card design, include a spot you would like to light up and also a 'press here' area. Colour it in however you like.

PRESS HERE

2

On the spot where you want to position the light, use a pin to create two small holes the same width apart as the legs on the LED.

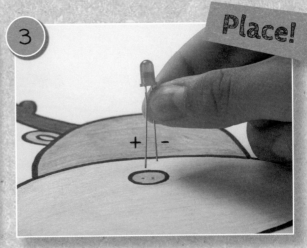

3 Place!

Now slot the LED into the two holes you've made, with the longer leg on the left and the shorter leg on the right.

4

Turn the card over and bend the legs out to secure. Notice that one of the legs on the LED is longer than the other – remember which one is longer, as this is the positive side.

LIGHT EMITTING DIODE

It is important to get your LED the correct way around for it to work! LEDs have a longer leg (positive) and a shorter leg (negative). The negative side also has a flat edge on the base of the bulb. LEDs come in a range of colours and sizes.

+   –

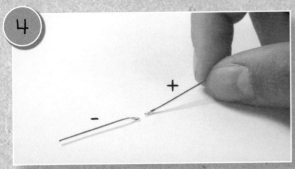

5 Cut!

Carefully cut two 10mm strips of foil.

6

Slide foil under one of the LED legs and fold the foil round until it covers the back of the 'press here' area. Use a glue stick to glue into place.

69

7 *Mark!*

Close the card and mark a point on the inside bottom face at the point right below the 'press me' area.

8

Carefully fold the other foil strip from the LED's other leg to the point you've just marked. Glue the foil in place.

How it works

When you close the card, the foil on the front and back sides touch, creating a full circuit for the electricity from the coil cell to pass round.

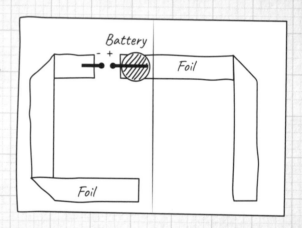

Battery

Foil

Foil

9

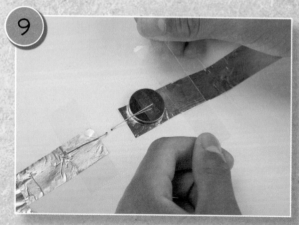

Place the coin cell between the foil and longer LED leg with the positive + side facing upwards. Secure both LED legs down with tape.

10 *Glue!*

Add some additional decoration, such as these googly eyes.

70

11

Test!

Close the card and try it out!

If your LED doesn't work

- Turning your coin cell over – you may have your positive and negative mixed up!

- Make sure your foil, LED legs and coin cell are secure so you don't get a loose connection.

- Ensure your two pieces of foil are continuous and not broken anywhere.

PRESS HERE

THE SCIENCE OF HOME HELPERS

LEDs

Light emitting diodes or LEDs are found in loads of everyday items such as your TV standby button as a single light, or clustered together to illuminate a traffic light. They use a lot less power than traditional light bulbs, and last much longer.

Solar power

Your night light only lights up at night. But how does it generate and store power during the day? It uses something called a photovoltaic cell to collect energy from the sun, then stores this in a small battery to use when it gets dark. Huge banks of these solar panels are already helping to power sunny countries. One day, this may be the world's cheapest and cleanest source of energy.

Inside a battery

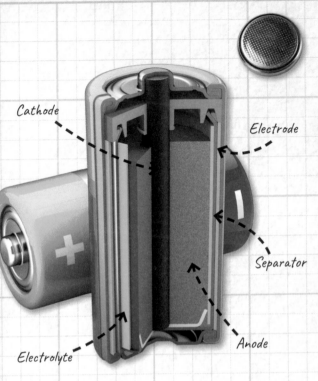

Cathode

Electrode

Separator

Anode

Electrolyte

We use batteries in so many of our everyday devices, but have you ever wondered what's inside? Batteries are made up of cells that contain three components: electrodes, an electrolyte and a separator. Each cell has two electrodes. A cathode connects to the positive end and an anode to the negative end. When the circuit is completed, a chemical reaction occurs in the battery which creates an electric current.

Conductivity

Did you know that other materials can be used to conduct electricity other than just wires and metal? Salt water is a good conductor and so are acidic liquids such as lemon juice or fizzy pop, but it is hard to get liquids to stay in one place. Try using play dough instead – the salt in the dough helps it to conduct electricity!

OUT & ABOUT

These great makes are perfect for taking with you on outdoor adventures!

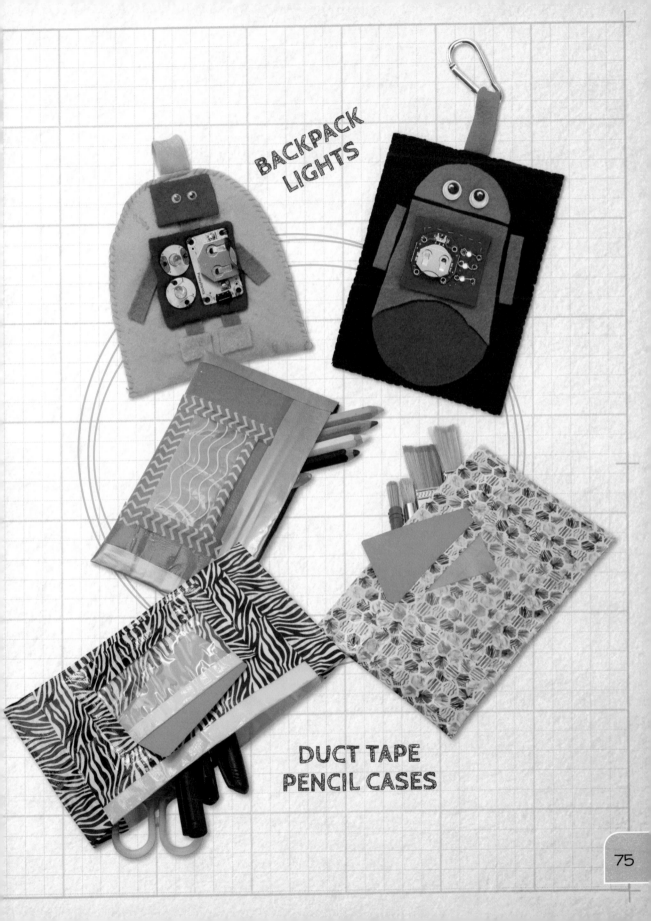

BACKPACK
LIGHTS

DUCT TAPE
PENCIL CASES

BACKPACK LIGHT

WITH A BIT OF SEWING AND CONDUCTIVE THREAD, YOU CAN MAKE THESE LIGHT-UP SHAPES TO HANG ON YOUR BACKPACK!

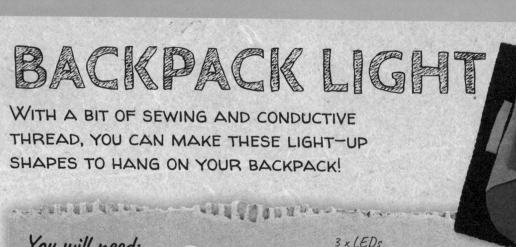

You will need:

Wobbly eyes

3 x LEDs

Sewing needle

Conductive thread

Sewing thread

Sewable battery holder

Coin cell battery

Key ring

Felt

Tools required:
- Needle-nose pliers
- Hot glue gun
- Cutting mat
- Scissors

1 Place a coin battery in the sewable battery holder.

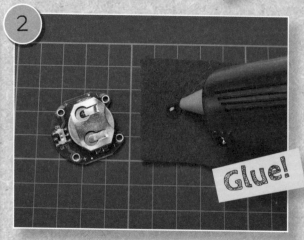

2 Cut a piece of felt approximately 50mm x 50mm. Use a small bit of glue to attach the battery holder on the left hand side.

Glue!

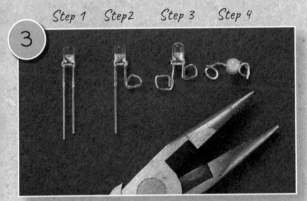

Step 1   Step2   Step 3   Step 4

Take an LED and notice one leg is longer than the other. This is the POSITIVE leg. Using a pair of needle-nose pliers, curl the long leg into a loop that stops a little way from the top of the LED. Then twist the looped legs so the LEDs can sit flat.

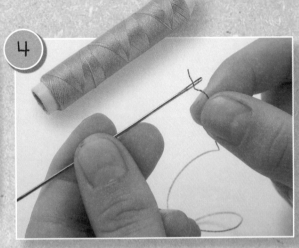

Thread a needle with about 300mm of conductive thread.

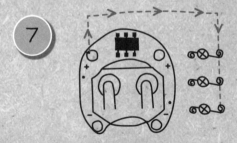

Sew loops around the POSITIVE (+) hole in the top left hand corner of the felt. To make a good connection, sew about 6 loops, pulling the thread tight each time.

Sew on the first LED by looping thread around the longer looped POSITIVE (+) leg three or four times, pulling tight each time to ensure a good connection. Don't sew the left side of the LED yet!

Repeat the process to sew in the second and third LEDs as shown. When you have sewn in the third LED, secure and cut the thead.

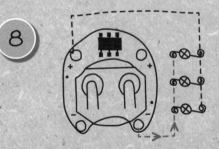

Start a new stitch on the NEGATIVE hole (-) and make connections in sequence to the NEGATIVE legs of the LEDs. When you reach the last LED, secure and cut the thread.

9 You should end up with a stitched circuit like this. Test the connection by switching it on!

Cut!

10 Cut two rectangles of felt in two different colours, and a thin strip in a third colour.

11 Place the two rectangles on top of each other. Using the black thread (not the conductive thread!) sew all the way around three sides.

12 Stuff the pouch with scraps of felt.

Loop!

13 Make a loop with the thin strip of felt and place it in the centre of the unstitched edge.

14 Put in a couple of stitches to secure the loop. Stitch all the way across to keep everything in.

15

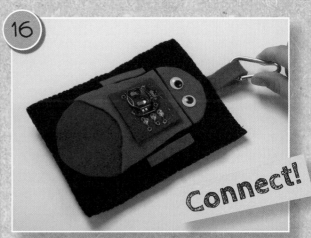

16

Connect!

You can now create any design you like. We've made a robot! You can either hot glue or stitch the felt pieces on to the pouch. Finally, add your circuit.

Finally add a hoop or hook to the loop so it can be secured to your backpack.

Here are some other designs you could try. The fish has an LED at the end of the pipe cleaner, and the switch in its mouth!

How it works

Conductive thread combines regular thread with a flexible conductive element like steel wire or silver. It's easily purchasable online. It's not cheap – but for projects like this, a little goes a long way!

79

DUCT TAPE PENCIL CASE

THIS PENCIL CASE IS GOOD-LOOKING, HARD-WEARING AND WON'T TAKE LONG TO MAKE!

You will need:

Tools required:
- Cutting mat
- Scissors
- Ruler
- Craft knife
- Pen

Duct tape and patterned tape – both in two different colours or designs

200mm zip seal bag

1

Cut a length of 200mm seal off the top of the zip seal bag. Save the rest of the bag for later.

Separate the two halves of the seal and lay them seal side up.

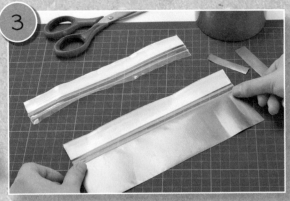

Cut a piece of 200mm long duct tape and stick it below the seal.

Turn the tape over and fold the seal back on itself.

Place it facing down with the sealed edge at the top. Cut a 200mm long peice of different coloured tape and stick to the first piece of tape to form the side of your pencil case.

Then repeat this with a second piece of tape.

Make up a second section using the other seal to form two identical pieces. Lay them opposite each other with the seals facing out.

8

Using the tape you started with, put a strip down the middle of both pieces to join them.

9

Use further strips of tape to cover the inside up to the seals. Be careful not to tape over the seals!

10

Seal!

Fold the pencil case in half and seal it.

11

Use thin strips of tape to seal the sides of the pencil case.

12

Take the remaining zip-seal bag and draw a rectangle 100mm x 60mm to form an ID pocket.

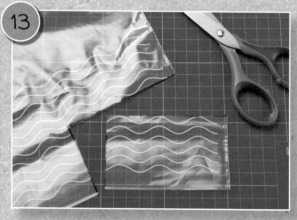

13

Cut it out with a pair of scissors.

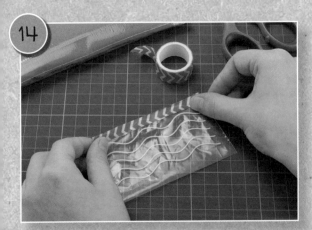

14

Seal the long open edge with a fun patterned tape.

15

Use thin strips of tape to secure the bottom and sides of the ID pocket.

Why not try different coloured tape combinations to make different designs? Then fill them up with pens and pencils!

THE SCIENCE OF OUT AND ABOUT

What is glue?

Glues are part of a larger family known as adhesives. While adhesives can be made from chemicals, glues are made from natural sources such as animal and fish bones, tree sap and even milk! Ancient tribes first discovered glue by processing animal bones, skin and hides and realised that the substance produced was sticky and useful for holding things together.

Why is duct tape so strong?

Duct tape is made from woven fibres that run vertically and horizontally, and then covered in a thin flexible plastic coating on one side and a sticky glue on the other. The fibres give it a lot of strength whilst keeping it flexible, but allow it to be easily torn into strips.

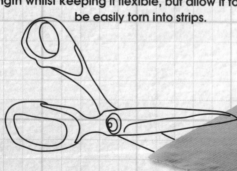

Wearable electronics

Wouldn't it be cool to have an invisible computer in your clothes? Scientists are working on ways to get electronics into all kinds of soft materials. Super fine filaments are coated with a very thin layer of silver before

being twisted together to form thread. This thread can be used to incorporate electrical components, such as lights, into fabric to create unique fashion items. Wearable technology is also being developed for health applications such as monitoring your heart rate or blood pressure through your clothes.

How are plastics made?

Plastic seems like a very artificial material - but did you know it's made from organic materials including oil, coal and even natural gas? The simple molecules in these substances are linked together to produce stable, hard-wearing molecules called polymers. However, because these types of polymers don't occur in nature, plastics can take a long time to break down, polluting our land and oceans. This is why it's so important to reuse existing plastic wherever possible.

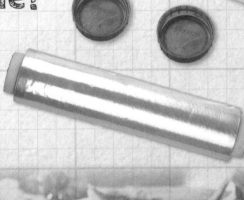

MINI-VERSE

All of these makes are
fantastic mini versions of much
larger real-life things!

MINI
FERRIS
WHEEL

MINI
BASKETBALL
GAME

MINI GEODESIC
GREENHOUSE

MINI GEODESIC GREENHOUSE

THIS GREENHOUSE WILL REALLY KEEP DELICATE
PLANTS WARM... PLUS IT LOOKS STUNNING TOO!

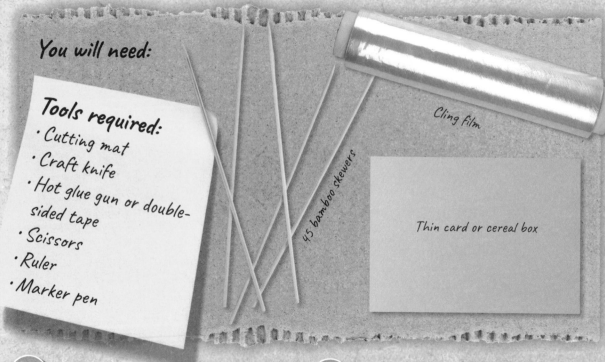

You will need:

Tools required:
- Cutting mat
- Craft knife
- Hot glue gun or double-sided tape
- Scissors
- Ruler
- Marker pen

45 bamboo skewers

Cling film

Thin card or cereal box

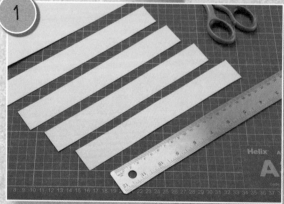

1

Cut card into 30mm wide strips.

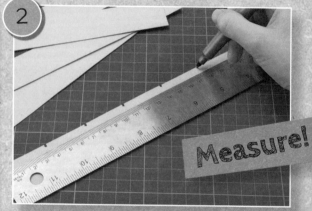

2

Measure!

Starting at the top left edge, measure 175mm and
make a mark. Then from this point make marks at
35mm intervals.

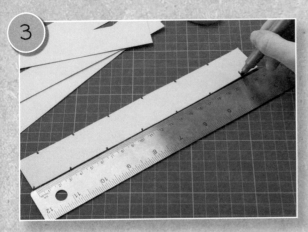

Starting at the bottom left edge, make marks intervals of 35mm.

Join the dots to form triangles.

Cut them out. Repeat this until you have 45 triangles.

Take three bamboo skewers and form a triangle. Place a card triangle under each corner. Using a hot glue gun, glue the skewer to the card.

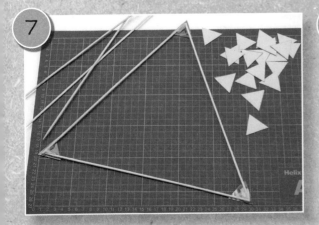

Repeat this process until you have 15 triangles.

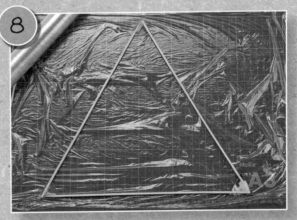

Roll out some clingfilm and lay a triangle on top.

9

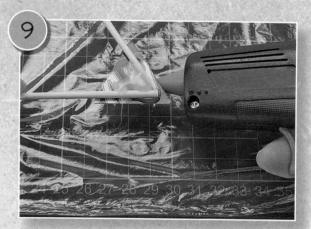

Carefully lift a corner and use hot glue or double sided tape between this and the clingfilm.

10

Ask an adult to help!

Repeat for the other two corners, pulling the clingfilm tight each time. Trim the clingfilm about 30mm from the skewer.

11

Wrap!

Fold the trimmed edge over the skewer to form a neat edge. Repeat this for all 15 triangles.

12

Lay two triangles next to each other along their sides and secure together with clear tape.

13

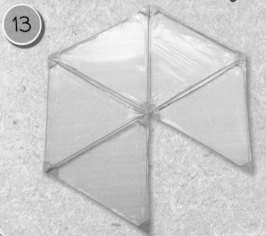

Add a further three triangles in a hexagon shape (leaving one space) and secure with clear tape.

14

Tape!

Raise the centre of the triangles to form a roof, bringing the remaining two sides together, and secure with tape.

15 Take five triangles and arrange them around the base of the roof section like a star and secure with tape.

16 Take the remaining five triangles. Place one to the left side of each of the previous five and secure with tape.

17 Carefully lift the centre of the roof and the remaining triangles will flop down to form the sides of the dome. Join the remaining triangles together to create your geodesic dome!

How it works

Your greenhouse will trap heat inside, but also let light in. It's perfect for growing plants that can only grow in hot cilmates!

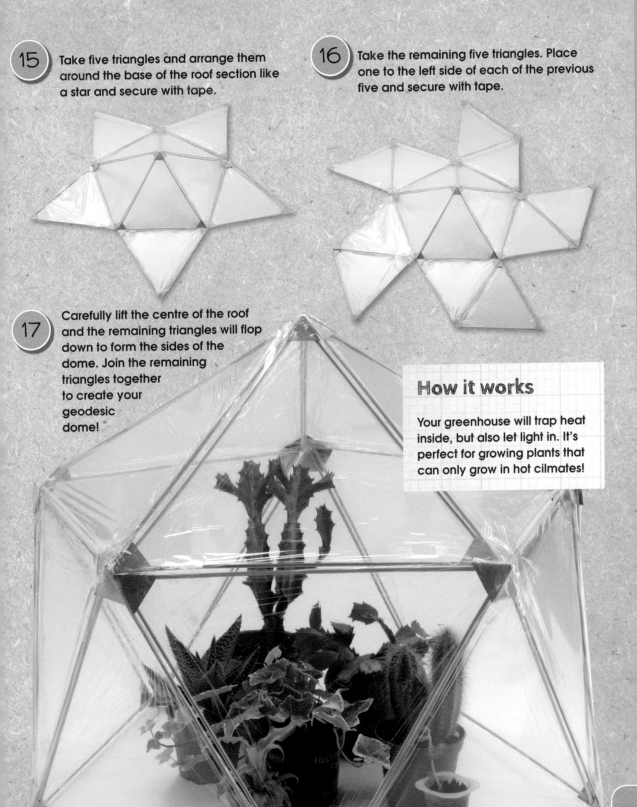

MINI BASKETBALL GAME

THIS GREAT MINI BASKETBALL GAME IS JUST LIKE THE ONES YOU MIGHT FIND IN AN AMUSEMENT ARCADE... ONLY SMALLER!

You will need:

Thin craft sticks

Milk bottle top

Elastic band

Wooden dowel

5x pieces of cardboard
350mm x 550mm

Thick craft sticks

Table tennis balls

Fruit netting

Tools required:
- Hot glue gun
- Cutting mat
- Marker pen
- Steel ruler
- Junior hacksaw
- Scissors

1

550mm

200mm

350mm

80mm

50mm

100mm 50mm 50mm

Take a piece of card to make the base of your game and mark on two ziz-zag lines using the following measurements.

2

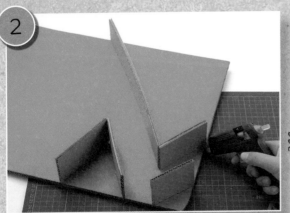

Take a second piece of card and cut strips 60mm high. Trim them to match the sections of your zig-zag lines and stick down with hot glue.

3

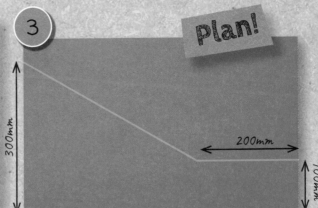

Plan!

300mm

200mm

100mm

Take two large pieces of card and draw out this shape on both.

4

Ask an adult to help!

Cut to the shapes out. These are the sides of your game.

5

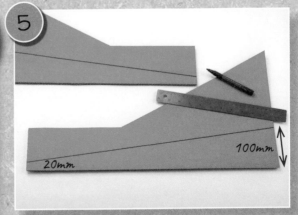

100mm

20mm

Draw a sloping line from approximately 100mm high at the back, to 20mm high at the front of your side pieces.

6

Use hot glue to attach the base to the sides along this line.

7

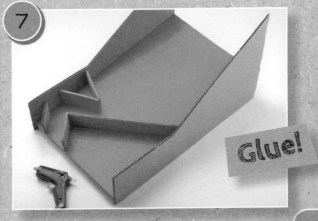

Glue!

You should have something like this.

93

8

From the piece of card you used to cut the zig-zags, cut a strip 100mm wide. Line it up with the bottom of the slope and mark the area at the base of the zig-zag, and then cut this area out.

9

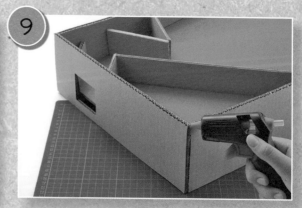

Use hot glue to fix the base piece in position.

10

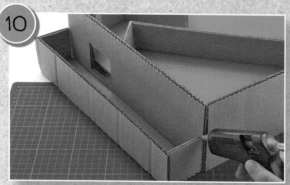

From the same card, cut two pieces of 50mm x 350mm and two pieces of 50mm x 50mm. Glue these together to form a two-sided trough, and glue this to the front of the game.

11

To make the hoops, take a plastic fruit net and cut off the ends and along the length to form a rectangle. Cut it into three strips approximately 70mm wide and 200mm long.

12

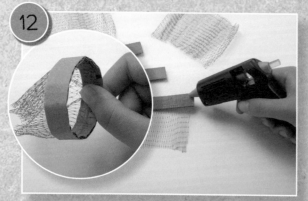

Cut a strip of card 200mm long and 10mm wide. Use glue to attach a piece of net to the card. Curl the strip into a hoop and secure with glue. Repeat two more times to make three hoops.

13

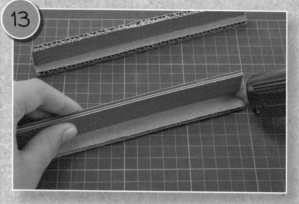

Cut four strips of card 200mm by 20mm. Stick two strips together into a T shape post, and repeat with the other two strips. Attach two of the hoops to the posts.

Using a spare piece of card, cut three rectangles approximately 100mm x 80mm and draw a smaller rectangle onto each one to form the backboards.

Glue two of the backboards onto the posts, then glue the hoop onto all three backboards.

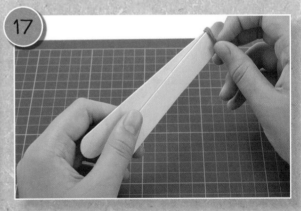

Use hot glue to secure one hoop onto the middle of the backboard and the two posts in front.

To make the ball launcher, take two wide craft sticks and tightly wrap two small elastic bands around one end.

Stack!

Use glue to stick four thin craft sticks together into a stack.

Slide the stack of thin craft sticks between the wide sticks and as close to the elastic bands as you can to form a catapult. Use hot glue to secure them in place, and glue on the bottle top.

95

20 Cut a piece of dowel about 50mm long.

Ask an adult to help!

21 Turn the catapult over and glue on a piece of dowel just below the halfway point.

22 Use a pencil or sharp point to pierce a hole for the dowel in the cardboard cover at the front of the game.

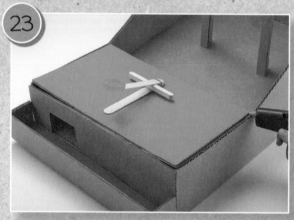

23 Use hot glue to secure the lid in place. Swivel the catapult to aim at the baskets.

24 Take a pack of table tennis balls (orange ones work best!) and use a black marker pen to draw on lines to resemble basket balls.

Your game is completed! Use the launcher to shoot the balls into the hoops. What's your high score?

MINI FERRIS WHEEL

THIS MASSIVE, MAGNIFICENT FERRIS WHEEL IS SURE TO GET GASPS OF AMAZEMENT FROM ALL YOUR FRIENDS!

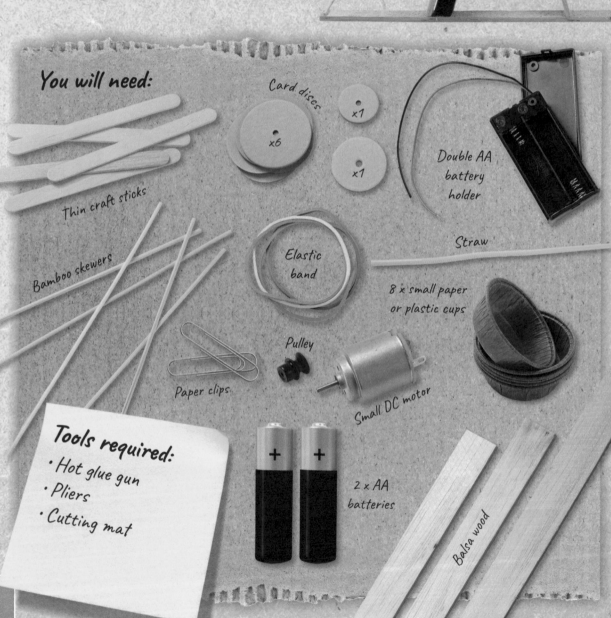

You will need:

Thin craft sticks

Card discs
x6
x1
x1

Double AA battery holder

Bamboo skewers

Elastic band

Straw

8 x small paper or plastic cups

Pulley

Paper clips

Small DC motor

Tools required:
- Hot glue gun
- Pliers
- Cutting mat

2 x AA batteries

Balsa wood

1 Trim 8 wooden skewers to 155mm in length and glue one onto a large card disc.

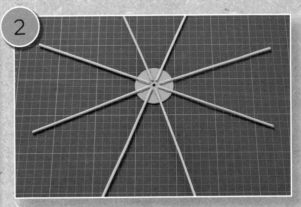

2 Glue the rest of the skewer at equal intervals to form the spokes of the wheel.

3 Cut 8 short lengths of craft stick…

4 …and glue one to the end of each spoke.

5 Glue a second card disc over the centre of the spokes.

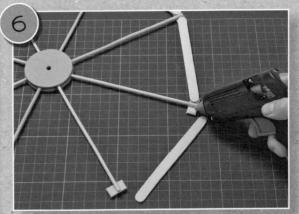

6 Lay craft sticks between the short sections at the end of each spoke to form the outer edge of the wheel, and secure with hot glue.

 7 Repeat steps 1-6 to create a second wheel.

8

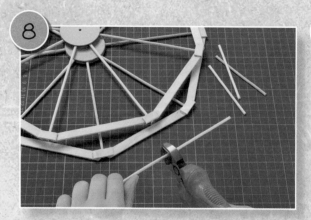

Cut 8 pieces of wooden skewer 100mm long.

9

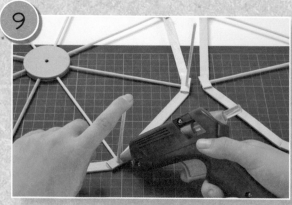

Glue one vertically to each of the short lengths of craft sticks on one of the wheels.

10

Turn the wheel over and place it on top of the second wheel. Line up the spokes and use hot glue to bond both wheels together.

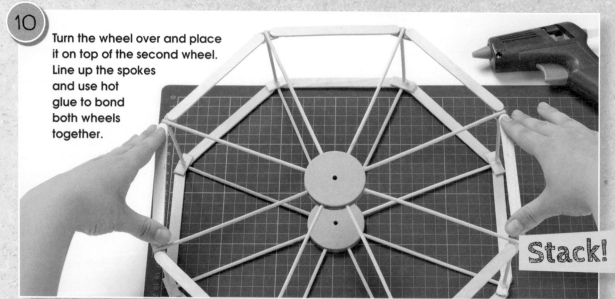

Stack!

11

Thread a skewer through the centre of both wheels...

12

...and fix into place using hot glue.

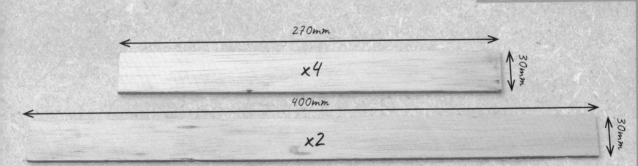

270mm
30mm
x4

400mm
30mm
x2

13 To build the frame, use balsa wood or thin card and cut two pieces at 30mm x 400mm and four pieces at 30mm x 270mm.

14

110cm

Take two of the shorter pieces and glue together in a V shape. Turn the V upside down and glue centrally onto one of the longer pieces to create a frame. Repeat this to create a second frame.

15

Glue a short piece of straw to the top of each frame. Place the frames either side of the wheel and thread the straw over the central skewer. The frame should sit a few millimetres away from each wheel.

16

Secure the two frames together by gluing a length of skewer between the frames at either end of the base.

17

Hook!

To make the seats for your Ferris wheel, take 8 small cups and use unfolded paperclips to create two hooks for each one. Hook one seat over each crossbar on the wheel.

18

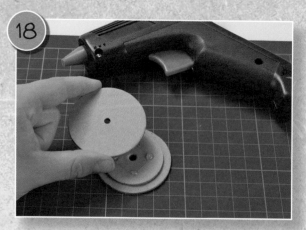

To motorise your Ferris wheel, make a card pulley by gluing together a medium card disc with two larger discs either side, as shown.

19

Fit the small plastic pulley to the motor.

20 Connect the battery pack to the motor by threading each wire through a point on the back of the motor and twist the wires to ensure a good connection.

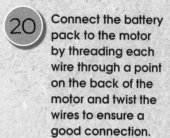

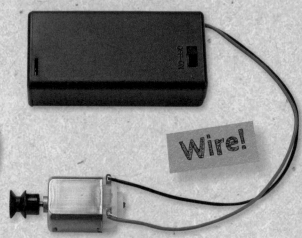

Wire!

21

Thread the pulley onto the central skewer and glue into place on the outside of the frame. Now wrap an elastic band around this and the larger card pulley.

22

Pull the band taut and glue the motor to the frame. Attach the battery pack to the frame, making sure you can still access the switch!

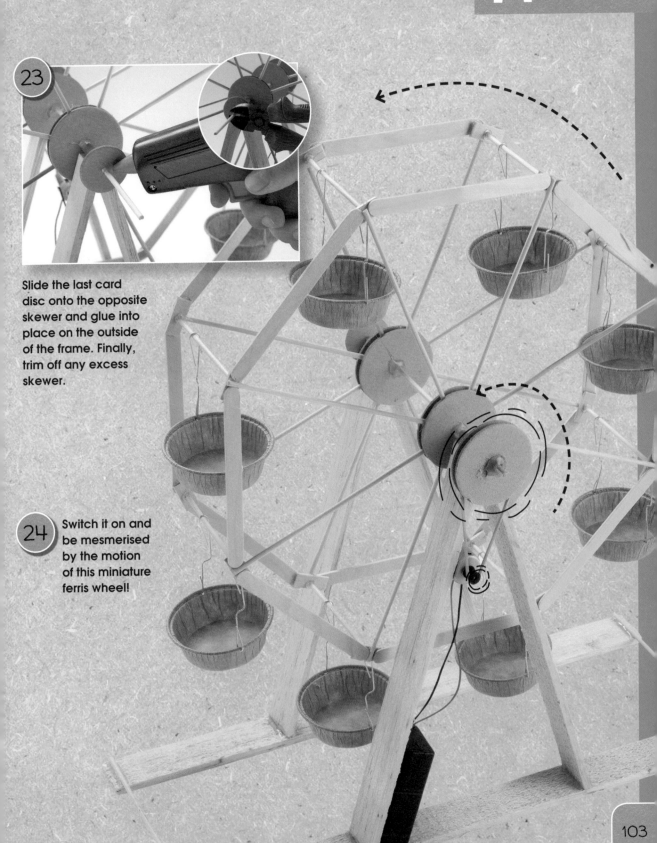

23

Slide the last card disc onto the opposite skewer and glue into place on the outside of the frame. Finally, trim off any excess skewer.

24 Switch it on and be mesmerised by the motion of this miniature ferris wheel!

THE SCIENCE OF MINI-VERSE

Mini-measurements

Our universe is made up of massive things such as galaxies, but also super-tiny things we can't even see, like atoms. Scientists measure atoms in nanometres, cells in micrometres, people in metres, mountains in kilometres and the sun in gigametres!

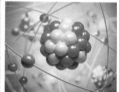 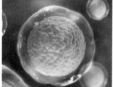   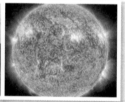

Nanometres (nm)   Micrometres (µm)   Metres (m)   Kilometres (km)   Gigametres (gm)

Self-contained ecosystems

The biosphere is the part of our planet where life exists. It extends up into the sky where birds and insects fly and down to the depths of the ocean and includes everything in between. You can create your own mini plant based ecosystem in a sealed jar called a terrarium. Terrariums don't need watering because they have their own mini water cycle too.

Catapults

Giant versions of the catapult in your basketball game were first used in battles to fire projectiles at the enemy. They are used today to help 'fire' aircraft from ships when they only have a very short runway. To make a projectile cover the most horizontal distance possible, it should be launched from a 45° angle.

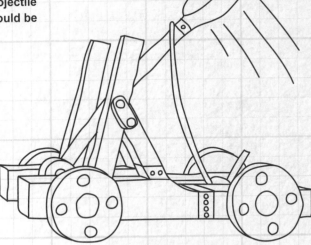

For your basketball net, you might need a smaller angle to allow the ball to travel higher and then fall into the net, rather than bouncing off the backboard. Experiment with which angle works best by adding or removing craft sticks.

Why do basketballs have bumps?

When basketball was first invented, it was actually played with soccer balls, but these were slippery and hard to keep hold of, which was a big problem. Scientists engineered a new ball, making it bigger and including hundreds of tiny bumps. These bumps increased the surface area which increased friction between the players hand and the ball, making it less slippery.

GLOSSARY

Aerodynamic
The design of a shape to help reduce the amount of drag as the object moves through the air.

Axle
The revolving shaft connecting a set of wheels.

Balsa wood
A super light but strong hardwood from a fast growing tree in Central and South America. Perfect for using in lightweight projects.

Bamboo skewers
Thin sticks with a pointy end made from bamboo. Used for making kebabs, but they make perfect lightweight axles too!

Bradawl
A woodworking hand tool shaped a bit like a screwdriver with a pointed end.

Cell
A single unit inside a battery, or a small coin-sized battery.

Conductive

Being able to conduct something – usually heat or electricity.

Corrugated

Cardboard is corrugated by adding a wiggly layer of card inside it to strengthen it.

Density

How much matter an object contains related to the size of the object.

Diameter

The measurement from one side of a circle to the other.

Dowel

A long, thin cylindrical piece of wood – often used for when an axle is needed.

Drill bit

The twisted metal piece that fits into a drill to form the hole. They come in different sizes and for different materials.

Electric circuit

A complete loop for electricity to flow around. It usually contains switches, lights and resistors or other electrical components.

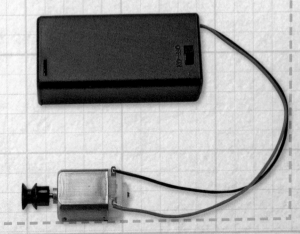

GLOSSARY

Gear
A wheel with teeth that fits together with another gear to change direction, speed or force.

Hydraulics
The use of liquids under pressure to help control machinery.

Insulator
Something that won't conduct electricity or heat.

LED
A light emitting diode is a semiconductor that emits light when electricity passes through it. A great energy-efficient light for electrical projects.

Pilot hole
A small hole usually made with a bradawl to help stop the drill bit from moving when drilling larger holes.

Pliers
A hand tool used for cutting or compressing materials.

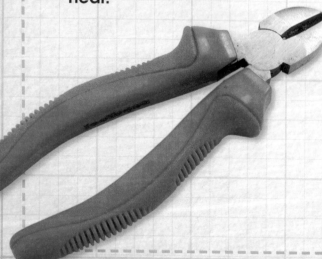

Pulley

A wheel with a central groove to guide a rope or string, used to lift heavy loads more easily.

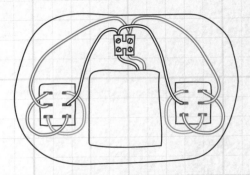

Wiring diagram

A clear drawing showing the components of an electrical circuit using simple shapes.

Terminal block

A plastic block used to connect wires together with a clamp, usually controlled using a small screwdriver.

Vice

A clamping device usually connected to a workbench used to hold an object still.

INDEX

YOUR NOTES

Use this page to plan projects
or jot down new ideas.